A Society of States

A Society of States

or

Sovereignty, Independence, and Equality in a
League of Nations

W. T. S. Stallybrass

Routledge
Taylor & Francis Group

First published in 1918 by George Routledge and Sons, Ltd.

This edition first published in 2018 by Routledge
2 Park Square, Milton Park, Abingdon, Oxon, OX14 4RN
and by Routledge
52 Vanderbilt Avenue, New York, NY 10017

Routledge is an imprint of the Taylor & Francis Group, an informa business

© 1918 by Taylor & Francis

Publisher's Note
The publisher has gone to great lengths to ensure the quality of this reprint but points out that some imperfections in the original copies may be apparent.

Disclaimer
The publisher has made every effort to trace copyright holders and welcomes correspondence from those they have been unable to contact.
A Library of Congress record exists under ISBN:

ISBN 13: 978-0-367-15169-0 (hbk)
ISBN 13: 978-0-367-15170-6 (pbk)
ISBN 13: 978-0-429-05544-7 (ebk)

W. T. S. STALLYBRASS

A SOCIETY OF STATES; OR, SOVEREIGNTY, INDEPENDENCE, AND EQUALITY IN A LEAGUE OF NATIONS

LEOPOLD CLASSIC LIBRARY

A SOCIETY OF STATES; OR, SOVEREIGNTY, INDEPENDENCE, AND EQUALITY IN A LEAGUE OF NATIONS

———

A SOCIETY OF STATES

A SOCIETY OF STATES

OR

SOVEREIGNTY, INDEPENDENCE, AND EQUALITY IN A LEAGUE OF NATIONS

BY

W. T. S. STALLYBRASS, M.A. (Oxon.)

FELLOW AND VICE-PRINCIPAL OF BRASENOSE COLLEGE,
OXFORD; OF THE INNER TEMPLE, BARRISTER-AT-LAW

"As far as the sovereignty of the States cannot be reconciled to
the happiness of the people, the voice of every good citizen must be,
Let the former be sacrificed to the latter."

—MADISON in *The Federalist.*

LONDON
GEORGE ROUTLEDGE & SONS, LTD.
NEW YORK: E. P. DUTTON & CO.

FIRST EDITION : *November,* 1918.

CONTENTS

III

IV

V

APPENDIX I

APPENDIX II

APPENDIX III

APPENDIX IV

PREFACE.

THE idea of a League of Nations has now taken firm root. The spade-work has been done. Leading statesmen of every country, in eloquent and glowing words, have proclaimed their adherence to the movement for its constitution after the war. It has extorted even the tribute paid to vice—hypocrisy. The seed has been sown. What manner of fruit it will bear will depend upon the knowledge and patience and care with which it is tended in its early growth.

The first task that lay upon those who believed that, through the co-operation of civilized States within a League, the world might win some respite from war and the threat of war, was to evangelize—to hammer away at their theme and announce their belief, in season and out of season, until a great body of opinion took shape, touched with their enthusiasm and filled

2

with their faith. Both the objects at which the League aims and the efficacy of the League to attain those aims now meet with a wide (if not a general) acceptance. The first task is accomplished.

The French say that our whole career depends upon our first step. But in the case of a League of Nations mere acceptance of the principle will not in itself guarantee success. The foundations must be truly laid. That can only be if the statesmen of the world bring to bear all the knowledge and ability of which they are possessed in settling the constitution of the League. Hitherto, with the exception of President Wilson, the statesmen have necessarily been so pre-occupied with the effective prosecution of the war that they have had little time or energy to consider the details of international reorganization. They have been as studiously vague as they have been eloquent in all their statements on the subject. Even the men to whose enthusiasm the movement owes its strength have been so concerned to gain acceptance of the general principle that they have devoted relatively little consideration to particular aspects of the problem. The amateur constitution-builder has been building on so large a scale that he has not had time to consider the plan in detail. Yet if the League is to achieve its aims, the details also will count. We must lie under no illusions as to the magic of a mere document; it will not be enough that the constitution of the League is accepted unless men believe, with conviction, in the principle which it embodies, and are ready to work whole-heartedly and, if necessary, to fight for that principle. It is no less true that generous enthusiasms and intellectual assent will not of themselves be sufficient to make the League a success if the constitution is not rightly framed. To rush into a League without full and careful preliminary investigation would be to invite disasters as bad as those from which we already suffer.

The time has now come when the numerous points which have to be settled before the idea can be given life should be carefully and impartially thrashed out one by one. The ground must be prepared for the statesmen; and part of that preparation lies in clearing our minds.

In this little volume I have endeavoured to deal with one small corner of the building.

In a book written nearly two years ago we are warned that " the first question which every Government will ask about the League will be: ' In what particular does it limit my sovereignty ? ' "[1] If an ordinary Englishman is told that under a League of Nations Great Britain will lose her independence, he will naturally refuse to accept a League of Nations as a proper or indeed even a tolerable solution of the present war. Again, if he is told that after the war Great Britain will have no more say in international difficulties than Paraguay, he is certainly not likely to become a supporter of the League. Yet he has been and he will be again told all these things. It is my object here to consider how far it is true that a State which joins a League of Nations will surrender its sovereignty or its independence, and to what extent all members of the League will be equal. In the name of these mystic words—sovereign-

---

[1] Brailsford, *A League of Nations,* ch. 1c, p. 309. So recently as October, 1918, Mr. Harold Spender speaks of the surrender of sovereignty as the " most formidable objection " to a League of Nations (*Contemporary Review,* p. 414).

ty, independence and equality—much false doctrine has been advanced, and in the discussions of these topics in connection with the proposed League of Nations there has been much muddled thinking and confused writing.

The roots of the present lie deep in the past; the future will be rooted in the present. You can no more take Society to pieces and by putting it together again create a new and different society than you can dismantle a Ford car and by assembling the parts again produce a Rolls-Royce. Human passions and inherited modes of thought, the desires and ideals of men, are not changed in a few years or even in a generation. Progress is slow : it comes by gradual modification and adaptation of existing institutions, not by pulling up by the roots all that has gone before. If, then, the result of our inquiry is to show that the union of civilized States in a League involves no violent change from the past—that a League of Nations is the natural super-structure to raise upon the edifice of the European State, it will *pro tanto* go to show that the path we are treading is leading in the right direction, and one along which we may hope to arrive at some real and permanent improvement in human relationships.

The sovereignty and independence of States is a conception common to international lawyers and to moral and political philosophers. Much of the difficulty of the subject arises from the fact that writers in these diverse fields have used the same terms to cover different conceptions. The lawyers try to describe international relations as they are; the philosophers limn them as they ought to be. In a discussion of the subject of this book we have to bear in mind both points of view—for a wise change must have both a necessary connection with the past and a real consistence with the end at which we aim.

I have, therefore, approached the topic in the following manner. After indicating the possible alternatives to a League of Nations—and the decisive argument for a League of Nations is that there seems to be no alternative which holds out any hope for the future of civilization —I state shortly the theory of the sovereign independent State in its logical perfection. I then examine the extent of the rights which, according to the practice of the statesmen and the beliefs of the international lawyers of the nineteenth century were believed to attach to the State as a result of its sovereignty, independence, and equality with other States. In other words the practical meaning of these words is explained. Only if we know what we have, can we know what we are losing. I next discuss to what extent, if at all, the conceptions of sovereignty, independence, and equality will undergo a change if a League of Nations is constituted, and conclude by a consideration of the relation of the proposed changes to the true purposes of State-existence.

Although I have a firm conviction in the need for the creation of a League of Nations and am inspired by a real hope that with a changed mind throughout the world it may achieve its purpose, I have not written as a partisan but dispassionately, in the sure belief that only honest and impartial discussion can be of use. Difficulties that are not faced now will only have to be met when it is too late. Nothing can be gained by not recognizing the facts. But the discussion is necessarily limited to the most authoritative schemes which have been put forward, and I have, therefore, for the most part confined myself to propositions which are applicable to those schemes. They will be found at the end of this volume. Where I have departed from this rule and have made observations applicable to the proposals of some only of the advocates of a League, I have tried to make this clear.

This little book makes no pretensions either to learning or to originality. It is, however, I hope, as clear and simple as is possible in view of the difficulty of a subject which is confounded by much abstract speculation and divergent practice; and attains, I hope, such substantial accuracy as is consistent with that clarity and simplicity at which I have aimed. Had I not been sometimes dogmatic when dogmatism was perhaps not justified and had I for the sake of formal accuracy qualified every statement made, the book would have been so overloaded with detail that my object would have been defeated. If any reader, who has not previously made a study of this subject, becomes as a result of reading it a little clearer in his ideas my purpose will have been attained.

I am greatly indebted to Mr. H. N. Spalding for the suggestions he made when the book was in manuscript; and to Dr. Hazel, of Jesus College, and Mr. A. J. Jenkinson, and Mr. R. W. Jeffery, of Brasenose College, for reading the proofs, the more so as they found time to do me this kindness whilst heavily engaged in labours directed to making possible the League of Nations by the triumph of our arms in the field.

Oxford,
October 1st, 1918.

A SOCIETY OF STATES

OR

Sovereignty, Independence and Equality in a League of Nations

INTRODUCTORY:
THE THREE ALTERNATIVES

WORLD-DOMINION : THE SOVEREIGN INDEPENDENT STATE : THE LEAGUE OF NATIONS

POLITICAL communities may regulate their relations to each other under any one of three possible systems. Two of these have been tried and have been found wanting; the third is now under the consideration of a distraught civilization.

The Middle Ages were dominated by the conception of a common superior before whose will States were to bow, whose commands they were to obey, and whose decisions upon differences between them they were to accept. That common superior Europe found first in the Roman Emperor, later in the Pope. In the Middle Ages from 1000 A.D. to 1500 A.D. the idea of right was the leading idea of statesmen; the period is characterized by the continued existence of small States; and medieval wars were as a rule wars of rights. But it must not be forgotten that "the imperial idea was," as Stubbs says,[1] "but a small influence compared with the superstructure of right, inheritance and suzerainty that legal instincts and a general acquiescence in legal forms had raised upon it." In the course of time quarrels, corruption, and obscurantism on the one side, a growing sense of nationality and a growing desire for freedom on the other, brought to an end such law and order as the Imperial and Papal supremacy secured.

After the Reformation came a new conception of the relation in which political communities stand to each other. We pass from a period in which the dominating influence is right to a period in which the dominating in-

[1] *Lectures on Medieval and Modern History*, lect. ix., p. 246.

fluence is force.[2] It was the birth of the State within the meaning of International Law. States were, according to this doctrine, sovereign, independent, and equal entities. Implicit in this conception is the belief that in international relations might is right; but over its naked horror, which may be seen best revealed in the works of modern German writers, Grotius, whose great book on the Law of War and Peace was published in 1625, and his successors threw a cloak of decency to which the name of International Law has been given. Decked out by jurists and increasingly obscured by custom, this underlying notion has yet been accepted by the civilized world from the Reformation until the present war.

During the last four years the cloak has been torn away. The scales have fallen from our eyes. The civilized world has been in travail, and hopes are rising high that of that travail will be born a new system of State-relationship —the Rule of Law. The phrase now usually employed to express these hopes is a League of Nations. The conception expressed in this

[2] *Ibid,* lectt. ix. and x.

phrase combines and reconciles that which is valuable and helpful in the idea of the sovereignty and independence of States with the existence of a common organ to act on behalf of those States for certain purposes.

The system of the Holy Roman Empire was a monarchy; the system of the last three hundred years was ill-disguised anarchy; the League of Nations will be a democracy, for it means the freedom and equality of States under the law. In a League of Nations every member will delegate to the League certain of the attributes of its sovereign power and its independence. The schemes for a League of Nations hitherto proposed for public consideration differ from one another in several respects; but this is a characteristic common to them all. It is admitted by most of those who place their hopes on such a League; it is raised as an objection by those who regard the notion of such a League with distrust or even repugnance.

So we find on the one side Mr. Wells' calling in aid the analogy of the indi-

---

[3] *In the Fourth Year*, ch. 3, p. 28.

vidual: "No man can join a partnership and remain an absolutely free man. You cannot bind yourself to do this and not to do that and consult and act with your associates in certain eventualities without a loss of your sovereign freedom"; and Sir Frederick Pollock[4] admitting that the convention by which the League of Nations is organized must depend for its binding force "on the renouncement by every party to it, in some measure, of independent sovereign power, and in particular of the right to be judge in one's own cause."[5] On the other side, the curious may be referred to M. Seignobos' article in *The New Europe* of April 4th, 1918, and Mr. Hilaire Belloc's in *The New Witness* of July 12th, 1918, as in-

---

[4] *The League of Nations and the Coming Rule of Law.*

[5] Lord Bryce's Group, however, in their " Proposals for the Prevention of Future Wars " speak of the League as " an association or union of independent and sovereign States," and definitely claim that existing States will retain their sovereignty. The articles of the Fabian Society's Draft Treaty invariably speak of the signatory States as " independent sovereign States," whilst in the introduction to the Draft Treaty it is claimed that " no impairment of sovereignty and no sacrifice of independence are proposed." This, however, seems clearly inconsistent with the statement on the next page that the establishment of a supernational authority is involved. Particulars of the chief schemes for a League of Nations may be found in *The Framework of a Lasting Peace*, edited by Leonard S. Woolf.

stances of the opposition to the League raised by its critics on this ground.[6] We are told that no political community careful of its honour or its prestige can surrender to an external body the functions proper to its sovereignty or its independence.

It is the object of these pages to establish two propositions. First, that the doctrine of the absolute sovereignty and independence of States, whilst in its day it met a need of the times and was an instrument of progress, no longer serves a useful purpose, for it is not in conformity with fact; secondly, that whilst the League of Nations does undoubtedly involve a rupture with the theories which have dominated the last three centuries, it does not involve so great a departure from the practice of the recent past as is sometimes supposed.

[6] *Cf.* J. B. Firth in *The Fortnightly Review*, September, 1918.

I. THE LOGICAL THEORY OF THE SOVEREIGN INDEPENDENT STATE

In the treaty made between Athens and Sparta in 421 B.C. one of the clauses provided that the Delphians should thenceforth " make their own laws, administer their own justice, and raise their own taxes."[1]   Grotius, the great Dutch jurist whose famous book already referred to has given him the reputation of being the Father of International Law, reminds us of the clause in the treaty of 421 B.C. when he is about to discuss the nature of sovereignty.[2] Unfortunately the idea of sovereignty is not limited to those attributes of self-government which were given to the Delphians.

The Germans are a logical people : their premises are often wrong, but no race has ever deduced more accurately the correct conclu-

[1] Thucydides, *History*, v., 18.
[2] *De Jure Belli et Pacis*, I., iii., 6, 1.

3

sions from *a priori* principles. It is not surprising, therefore, that we must turn to the German political philosophers to find the logical perfection of the doctrine of the sovereign independent State. Frederick the Great gave the world an illuminating example of the practical application of the doctrine. Hegel, breaking away from Kant's pacificism, laid a philosophic foundation for the dogma which places the State above all moral restrictions. The seed was sown in fruitful soil. We are now reaping the fruits of the Hegelian philosophy.[3] Of the many Germans who developed this particular side of Hegel's teaching none probably has had a wider influence over modern German thought than Treitschke. Treitschke knew something of international law, and was certainly less extreme in his views than many of his disciples. The logical conclusions which can be and have been drawn from the State-sovereignty theory, and which are generally accepted in Germany, may there-

---

[3] Even in England we find the Hegelian, Professor Bosanquet, absorbing Hegel's dangerous teaching on the non-morality of the State.

fore be fairly shown in the following extracts from Treitschke's most important book *Politik:*

" Since it is impossible to imagine a higher judge set above the States, which by their very nature are supreme, it is impossible that the necessity for war should be driven out of the world by force of argument. . . . Even among civilized nations, war is still the only form of lawsuit by which the claims of States can be asserted. . . . Every State will for its own sake limit its sovereignty to a certain extent by means of treaties. When States conclude agreements with one another, they do to some extent restrict their powers. But this does not really alter the case, for every treaty is a voluntary self-limitation of an individual power, and all international treaties contain the proviso: *rebus sic stantibus.* One State cannot hamper the exercise of its free will in the future by an obligation to another State. The State has no supreme judge placed above itself, and therefore it concludes all its treaties with that mental reservation.[4] This is confirmed by the fact that, so long as there is

[4] So Machiavelli: " A prudent ruler ought not to keep faith when by so doing it would be against his interest, and when the reasons which made him bind himself no longer exist." (*The Prince*, ch. 18). Hence in part no doubt Treitschke's admiration for Machiavelli. This detestable doctrine was also propagated by the Portuguese Jew, Spinoza.

an International Law, the moment that war is declared all treaties between the belligerent nations are cancelled. Now every sovereign State has the unquestionable right to declare war when it so desires; and therefore it is possible for every State to cancel its treaties. . . . The highest moral duty of a State is to maintain its power.[5] . . . The State is the supreme human community; therefore, in the case of the State, there can be no duty of self-sacrifice. . . . For one State to sacrifice itself in the interests of another would be not only immoral, it would be contrary to that principle of self-preservation, which is the highest duty of a State. . . . Even in its intercourse with other States, the preservation of its sovereignty is still the highest duty of the State. The enduring provisions of International Law are those which do not affect sovereignty, that is to say, those concerned with ceremonial and with international private law.

---

[5] It may be thought that Treitschke's admission that the State has a " moral duty " traverses my statement that the State is, according to these German thinkers, non-moral or above all moral restrictions. To speak of the " moral duty " of power is, however, a misuse of words. It is only by a metaphor that we can speak of the " moral duty " of the octopus to live; it is no less metaphorical to say that " the highest moral duty of the State is to uphold its power " (*Politik*, i., 100), or to affirm that " repudiation of its own power is, so far as the State is concerned, equivalent to the sin against the Holy Ghost." (*Ibid*, i., 34). It is a singular tribute to the universal claims of morality that almost without exception the votaries of Force invoke the support of Right and Duty, Justice and Honour in spite of the patent contradiction.

. . . A State must have a very highly-developed sense of honour if it is not to be disloyal to its own nature. The State is not a violet blooming in the shade. Its power must stand forth proud and refulgent, and it must not allow this power to be disputed, even in matters of forms and symbols. . . . No State in the world is to renounce that egotism which belongs to its sovereignty.[6] . . . The inalienable kernel of sovereignty lies legally in the authority to determine the scope of one's own rights of sovereignty, and politically in the appeal to arms.'"[7]

Such were Treitschke's opinions; such were the opinions of most German writers. If any doubt it, let him read the extracts from Adolph Lasson and others collected in the Introduction to Dr. J. B. Scott's book on *A Survey of International Relations between the United States and Germany, 1914-1917.*[8]

According to this doctrine because the State is sovereign it has the right to make and unmake, call in aid or disregard the law; because it is independent it has the right to carve out

---

[6] These translations are taken from Mr. H. W. C. Davis's admirable book, *The Political Thought of Heinrich von Treitschke*, pp. 151-178.

[7] *Politik*, i., 39.   [8] Pp., l.-lxx.

its own destiny and pursue its own ends without thought or observance of the like right in other States. The ethics of international morality resolve themselves into

> " The good old rule, the simple plan,
>   That they should take who have the power
>   And they should keep who can." [9]

As Hobbes said[10] many years ago "in all times kings and persons of sovereign authority, because of their independency, are in continual jealousies and in the state and posture of gladiators, having their weapons pointing and their eyes fixed on one another, that is, their forts, garrisons and guns, upon the frontiers of their kingdoms, and continual spies upon their neighbours : which is a posture of war." The whole of Hobbes' description of the relation of man to man in his imaginary state of nature is an admirable picture of the relation of State to State according to this doctrine. Man in the state of nature, he says, makes

---

[9] *Cf.* Rümelin (*Ueber das Verhältniss der Politik zur Moral : Reden und Aufsätze*, vol. i., p. 161) : " The preservation of the State justifies every sacrifice and is superior to every Commandment."

[10] *Leviathan*, ch. 13.

aggression upon man either because two men want the same thing, or because one man is afraid that another will attack him first, or to preserve his self-esteem. The three principal causes of quarrels therefore are competition, diffidence (i.e., distrust), and glory. " To this war of every man against every man this also is consequent that nothing can be unjust. The notions of right and wrong, justice and injustice, have there no place. Where there is no common power, there is no law; where no law, no injustice." And his conclusion is that in a state of nature the life of man is "solitary, poor, nasty, brutish and short."

The views so lucidly presented by Treitschke are the logical corollary to the theory that States are sovereign and independent units, and it is the working of these views in practice which we may observe if we look at Prussian State-craft and diplomacy[11] and the Prussian methods of waging war either under Frederick

[11] Diplomacy had its birth with the sovereign independent State. Prussian diplomacy to-day reminds us of Stubbs' statement (*op. cit.*, lect. x., p. 269) that diplomacy was " in its beginning a sort of *Kriegspiel*, in which threats and bribes on paper took the place of mobilisation and marches, sieges and invasions."

the Great or in the twentieth century. If the State is supreme and independent, it logically follows that the preservation of its sovereignty entire and its aggrandisement at the expense of other States are its chief end, and that treaties are only one means to that end; force and fraud are other means to the same end and militarism and dishonest diplomacy are enthroned; "honour" means, not honesty or chivalry or justice, but wide territories and a dominating trade and an armed force which shall strike terror into the hearts of all possible rivals. We may well apply to the philosophy of international relations held by the German school the expression "reasoned savagery" which Huxley in his famous Romanes Lecture used of the political philosophy of fanatical individualism.[12]

---

[12] *Evolution and Ethics,* p. 115.

II. THE CUSTOM AND PRACTICE
OF CIVILIZED NATIONS

ALL nations, however, are not so clear-headed or so logical as the German. Most writers of other nations, and some Germans, have not carried the theory of sovereignty to its logical extreme. "No custom," it has been said, "is ever a pure mistake, as is the case with many theories, and with the doctrines which rest on them."[1] No matter how loudly professors and statesmen have proclaimed the theory of the absolute independence of States, custom has always rejected it. The whole structure of so-called Private International Law has been built up in spite of this theory of independ-

[1] Lorimer, *Institutes of the Law of Nations*, vol. i., p. 28.

ence.[2]   It is upon the custom and usage of
nations that most English writers have based
their views of International Law without an
over-nice respect for logical consistency.   If
we wish to understand where things stood in
1914 we must understand the views generally
held outside Germany at that date.   I propose
therefore to state and examine as summarily
as is consistent with substantial accuracy the
usually accepted rules and principles of International Law bearing on the question of State-
independence.

That those States which are recognized as
members of the family of nations are sovereign,
independent, and equal is an assumption which
underlies almost all that has been written upon
International Law, and by many writers that

[2] When a child is born in America to an Englishman the *jus
soli* declares the son an American ; the *jus sanguinis* declares him
an Englishman.   Each country may according to its own laws
claim him as its subject.   When a Frenchman owns property in
England it may become necessary on his death to decide whether
the property descends according to the French or English law ;
when a Spaniard, resident in Germany, becomes bankrupt the
question arises as to whether Spanish or German law is to be applied, and what recognition one State will give to the application
of the law of the other.   A contract may be entered into in Austria
between a Dutchman and a Greek to be performed in Japan, and
enforcement of it may be sought in the American Courts.   Which
law applies?   The resolution of these and like " conflicts of law "
arising from the intercourse of modern independent States is the
domain of " Private International Law."

assumption has been regarded as an essential and fundamental postulate. So Halleck,[3] the American general whose book on international law may be found on every British warship, calls "the independence of sovereign States the true basis of international jurisprudence." But law must be in conformity with fact; and it is very clear that States are not in fact equal in every respect. It is scarcely more true that States are sovereign or independent in an absolute sense. International jurists have recognized this, and have overlaid the postulate of sovereignty, independence, and equality with so many exceptions and provisos that the words have acquired for publicists a very different meaning from that which they bear in their primary sense. We must endeavour, therefore, to ascertain what is the meaning to international lawyers in its practical application of each of these three terms.

§ I. THE MEANING OF SOVEREIGNTY

An eminent Oxford historian recently wrote in a letter to *The Times*:[4] "Sovereignty is a

---

[3] *International Law* (4th ed.), ch. I., vol i., p. 7.
[4] Ernest Barker: June 28th, 1918.

definition, not a thing." But the definition needs defining. "Sovereignty," says Wheaton,[5] the great American publicist, "is the supreme power by which any State is governed. This supreme power may be exercised either internally or externally. Internal sovereignty is that which is inherent in the people of any State or vested in its ruler, by its municipal constitution or fundamental laws. . . . External sovereignty consists in the independence of one political society in respect to all other political societies."

Or, in the better known language of John Austin,[6] a sovereign power is one to which the generality of a given society renders habitual obedience (the positive or internal side of sovereignty) and which is not itself habitually obedient to any determinate human superior (the negative or external side).

Although it is true, as Maine[7] pointed out, that in Austin the two conceptions of an In-

[5] *Elements of International Law* (8th ed.), Pp. 31-2.
[6] *The Province of Jurisprudence Determined,* Lect. vi. (3rd edition), p. 241.
[7] *The Early History of Institutions,* Lect. xii., p. 348.

dependent Political Society and of sovereignty are interdependent and inseparable from one another, the difference between external and internal sovereignty is of the greatest importance. Internal sovereignty belongs to the organ to which the people delegates its sovereignty; external sovereignty is the possession of the people itself,[8] though the ruler or sovereign of a State is, in international law, sometimes considered as representing, in his person, its sovereign dignity.[9] With internal sovereignty international law is not directly concerned; internal sovereignty will not be directly affected by the constitution of a League of Nations; it is the theory of external sovereignty alone which will have to undergo some modification if the League is brought into existence.[10]

It is fortunately therefore not necessary to traverse the arid wilderness which has been

[8] Bryce, *Studies in History and Jurisprudence*, vol. ii., Essay 10.
[9] Halleck, *ubi supra*, vol. i., ch. 5, p. 129.
[10] The theory of the internal as well as of the external sovereignty of the State is threatened at present. The Guild-Socialists and the High-Churchmen in England, the Syndicalists in France are all attacking the sovereignty of the State from within : see Ernest Barker's *Political Thought in England from Spencer to To-day*.

created by political philosophers and constitutional lawyers in discussing the why, the wherefore, and the what of internal sovereignty. But even from the point of view of the international lawyer the conception of sovereignty cannot be properly understood without some knowledge of the circumstances in which it originated and the history of its development. For from those origins and from that development it takes its present form.

In the days of the great Roman jurists the sovereignty of the Roman Emperor was theoretically supposed to have been derived from and delegated to him by the Roman people. It is from a later period that the traditional notions of sovereignty come. The traditional theory of sovereignty had its beginnings in an age of monarchs and oligarchies. It took its territorial character from feudalism. In the Dark Ages at first the only sovereignties in existence were, on the one hand, the sovereignty of the chiefs over their tribes, such as the Franks and the Lombards, and, on the other, the world sovereignty of the Emperor of Rome. In 987 A.D. the King of the Franks became the

King of France; sovereignty began to be associated with the proprietorship of a limited portion of the earth's surface. Sovereigns were feudal lords.[11] Sovereignty and property, in reality distinct, were confounded in an impenetrable haze.[12] Subjects were regarded as part of the patrimony of their rulers to be alienated as such without consultation or consent. The will of the sovereign was a will imposed upon the people. "The States," as Treitschke said, "have not issued from the sovereignty of the people, but were created against their will."[13] In the days when Bodin and Grotius and Hobbes wrote the sovereign represented the people not, as in England now, in the sense that whatever the people will becomes the will of the sovereign, but in the sense that whatsoever he willed became their will.[14] Austin's analysis of sovereignty in relation to the English and American constitutions of the nineteenth century is a brilliant *tour de force*. But the representative Government of a free people

---

[11] Maine, *Ancient Law,* ch. 4.
[12] Westlake, *International Law: Peace,* ch. 5.
[13] Treitschke, *Politik,* i., 113.
[14] Sir Leslie Stephen, *Hobbes,* ch. 4, p. 204.

cannot without violence be cast into the strait-jacket of the medieval notion of sovereignty.[15] It is scarcely less difficult to adapt the medieval notion of sovereignty to the changed circumstances of international intercourse.

§2.   THE "RIGHTS" OF SOVEREIGNTY

In the language of the Civilians the sovereign dignity of the State was *majestas;* the parts of its sovereign power were spoken of as *majestatis jura,* the rights belonging to and constituting that sovereign dignity.   We can only understand the real meaning of *majestas* if we know what are the *majestatis jura:* we can only understand the real meaning of external sovereignty if we know the rights which belong to a State because it is sovereign. Neither the definitions of the lawyers nor a study of historical origins alone will leave us with a clear conception of what sovereignty in

---

[15] This is seen by Professor Jethro Brown amongst others. " It seems probable," he says (*Austinian Theory of Law,* p. 286), " that the Jurisprudence of a near future will recognize that the State itself is the true sovereign, and that such a body as the Parliament of Great Britain should be described, not as the sovereign, but as the sovereign-organ."

international law in the twentieth century means. We must now therefore to achieve our purpose examine the so-called "rights" of sovereignty.

A State by virtue of its sovereignty has an exclusive authority over all persons, things, and acts within its territory or on its ships upon the high seas. That is to say, it and it alone can legislate for its own dominions; it and it alone can act as judge and enforce its decrees within them. Over its own subjects it exercises some personal jurisdiction even when they leave its territory. Each of these rights betrays clearly the feudal idea—the one tracing back to the territorial basis of feudalism, the other to the allegiance of the man to his lord.

The so-called rights of sovereignty are sometimes treated as rights attaching to independence, but of this more anon.[16]

§3. MODIFICATIONS OF THE "RIGHTS" OF
SOVEREIGNTY

Usage has, however, made certain inroads into the full rights of sovereignty.

[16] See below, p. 41.

4

The conflict which may arise between the territorial jurisdiction of one State and the personal right of jurisdiction of another State has given birth to the body of rules which is usually known as Private International Law. Those rules are in fact merely " the concessions and relaxations of sovereign right " which are usually admitted by civilized States.[17]

But it is not only in the sphere of Private International Law that we find modifications of and qualifications upon the rights of sovereignty.

Chief Justice Marshall, when delivering the opinion of the Supreme Court of the United States in the case of *The Schooner Exchange* in an elaborate and famous judgment, stated three exceptions to the full and complete power of a nation within its own territories. The foundation of each of these limitations upon national jurisdiction, he was careful to point out, must be traced to the consent, express or implied, of the nation itself. Otherwise they would imply a diminution of sovereignty to the

[17] Hall, *International Law* (7th ed.), pt. I., ch. 2, § 10, p. 52. See also above, p. 26.

extent of the restriction, and an investment of that sovereignty ·to the same extent in that power which could impose such restrictions. The three cases are : the exemption of the person of a sovereign from arrest or detention within a foreign territory, the immunity given to foreign ministers, the waiver of jurisdiction over the troops of a foreign prince allowed to pass through the dominions and over the national ships of war of a friendly power, entering a port open for their reception.[18]

Again it is generally admitted that a limit is set upon the right of the territorial sovereign to deal with the foreigner resident within his dominions. The resident alien may be made amenable to taxation, he may be called upon to perform police duties, but he cannot rightly be embodied in the naval or military forces of the State.[19] Hence the many conventions made between the Entente States during the present war for the enlistment of allied aliens. Even Germany in the early days of the war recog-

---

[18] Cranch's *Reports*, p. 116.
[19] T. A. Walker, *Manual of Public International Law*, Pt. ii., ch. 3, § 19 (1).

nized this.   A Rhodes scholar at Oxford, of
German ancestors but American citizenship,
happened to be spending his vacation in Germany when war broke out.   He tells of the
following experiences.   He spoke German
fluently, and was immediately seized for service
by the military who believed him a German,
and would not credit his protestations that he
was an American.   As he was being marched
through the streets of a German town, his
imagination still vivid and his mind not yet
tutored to the circumstances of war, he believed
that he was on the way to the Eastern front:
he saw the American Consulate, broke the
ranks and took refuge.   On establishing his
nationality he was assisted to leave the country.
Similarly during the American Civil War the
British Government addressed several effective
remonstrances against the compulsory enrol-
ment of British citizens resident in the United
States who had not been naturalized.

There are limitations also upon the State's
jurisdiction over ships under its flag.   Piracy,
that is, acts of violence done by a body of

men acting independently of any politically organized society,[20] is justiciable anywhere. And in wartime the neutral who wishes to trade overseas with a belligerent must submit to infringements of his sovereign rights which have been described[21] as " onerous and humiliating " and which are certainly extensive. He must suffer his merchant vessels to be visited and searched. If they try to enter a blockaded port he cannot complain if they are condemned as prize. If a neutral merchantman carries a cargo of goods destined for a belligerent even to the port of another neutral, and those goods have been declared contraband by the other belligerent (for it is the belligerent who decides what shall and what shall not be contraband), ship and cargo, if captured, will be adjudicated upon by the Courts of the aggrieved belligerent, and in some cases condemned, and the neutral State must watch its citizen lose ship and cargo without just cause of protest.

[20] Hall, *op. cit.,* Pt. ii., ch. 6, p. 71.
[21] Brailsford, *A League of Nations,* ch. 7, p. 206.

§4.   THE MEANING OF INDEPENDENCE

We now must try to find exactly what we
mean when we speak of States as independent.
Clearly we do not mean that the Sovereign
State lives in isolation.   It is no truer of the
State than the individual that

> "In the sea of life enisled,
>   With echoing straits between us thrown,
>   Dotting the shoreless watery wild,
>   We mortal millions live alone."

In 1711 that characteristic Englishman, Joseph
Addison, wrote after a visit to the Royal Exchange : " Nature seems to have taken a particular care to discriminate her blessings among
the different regions of the world, with an eye
to this mutual intercourse and traffic among
mankind, that the natives of the several parts
of the globe might have a kind of dependence
upon one another and be united together by
their common interest."[22]   Long before 1914 it
would have been truer to say of the members
of the family of nations that they were *inter*-
dependent than that they were *in*dependent in

22 *The Spectator*, No. 69.

the ordinary sense of the word. Full independence is inconsistent with relations. *A fortiori* it is inconsistent with the existence of law. A man who is a law to himself cannot be said to live under the law. There can be no need for international law if there are no international relations.

John Austin described[23] an independent political society as one which was not merely a limb or member of another political society. Hall defines[24] independence as "the power of giving effect to the decisions of a will which is free, in so far as absence of restraint by other persons is concerned," whilst Halleck found[25] the essential qualities of independence in "the right of will and judgment and the full capacity to contract obligations." But the definitions of the lawyers help us here even less than in the case of sovereignty.

§5. THE "RIGHTS" OF INDEPENDENCE

If we wish to discover and understand the meaning of independence, we must examine

---

[23] *loc. cit.*, p. 227.
[24] *Op. cit.*, Pt. i., ch. 2, § 10.
[25] *Op. cit.*, vol. i., ch. 3, p. 77.

rather the rights which are supposed to attach to a State because of its independence; for "independence does not at all mean boundless liberty of action."[26] "Every State," says Wheaton,[27] "has certain sovereign rights to which it is entitled as an independent moral being." These rights may be summarized as follows:—

(1) The right to self-preservation. This includes the right of self-defence, and that defence may take the form of preventing as well as of repelling an attack. As a means to self-preservation a State has the right to erect fortifications, levy troops, and maintain naval forces, uncontrolled, and the exclusive right to use troops in its own territory.

(2) The right to increase its national dominions, wealth, population, and power by all innocent and lawful[28] means.

---

[26] Oppenheim, *International Law*, Pt. i., ch. 1, § 97, p. 149.

[27] *Op. cit.*, p. 89. Wheaton treats as distinct the conditional international rights to which sovereign States are entitled, i.e., those to which they are only entitled under particular circumstances, for example, in a state of war. The distinction is unreal, for the rights of war flow from the right of self-preservation.

[28] This clearly makes the statement as meaningless as it is safe: it begs the whole question.

(3) The right to monopolize its own trade and to grant special privileges to other nations.

(4) The right to establish, alter or abolish its own internal constitution and to choose its rulers as well as its form of government.

(5) The right to prohibit the introduction of foreigners on its territory, and to expel them when they are there.

(6) The right to territorial inviolability.

(7) The right to make treaties or alliances with whom it will.

And in addition the so-called rights of sovereignty and of equality may with equal propriety be treated as rights of independence. We have already seen[29] that in Austin the notion of an Independent Political Society and the notion of sovereignty are interdependent, and that Wheaton defines external sovereignty as independence. How difficult it is to distinguish between sovereignty and independence or to think clearly about either will be realized by any one who cares to take the trouble to compare the statements made by

[29] Above, p. 29.

Halleck on this subject. We are first told that " the mere fact of dependence does not prevent a State from being regarded in international law as a separate and distinct sovereignty, capable of enjoying the rights and incurring the obligations incident to that condition,"[30] and that the sovereignty of a particular State is not necessarily destroyed either by mere nominal obedience to the commands of others or even by an habitual influence exercised by others over its councils.[31] But if by political organization or treaties of unequal alliance or protection, a State has parted with its rights of negotiation and treaty and has lost its essential attributes of independence, it can no longer be regarded as a sovereign State.[32] Yet we are a little later informed that " the very fact of the sovereignty " of the sovereign State " implies its independence of the control of any other State ";[33] that by reason of its independence it may exercise all rights incident to its sovereignty as a separate, distinct, and independent society; and that these rights are

[30] *International Law* (4th Edition), vol. i., ch. 3, p. 71.
[31] *Ibid*, p. 72. [32] *Ibid*, p. 74. [33] *Ibid*, ch. 4, p. 100.

limited only by the Law of Nature and the existence of similar rights in others. Independence is however free from the historical connexions which still cling to the word sovereignty, and so we find that Austin speaks of the independence of the nation and of the sovereignty of the Government.[34]

It is difficult to see how restrictions can be imposed upon external sovereignty which are not also restrictions upon independence. But the common practice, which I have followed, is to associate those rights which flow directly from the territorial character of sovereignty and the allegiance due to the Sovereign with sovereignty, and to treat all other rights as flowing from independence. The dichotomy is not however scientific.

§6. 'MODIFICATIONS OF THE "RIGHTS" OF INDEPENDENCE

At first sight the State to whom these rights attach would indeed seem to be untrammelled and independent almost in the fullest

---

[34] *Cf. loc. cit.*, pp. 235, 264.

sense. But theory and practice have alike hedged about these rights with modifications and exceptions. The Grotian theory of International Law was based upon a belief in the existence of a Law of Nature, and Grotius himself denied to the sovereign the right to do acts repugnant to the Law of Nature or the Law of God. For Grotius recognized that his system was a compound of law and ethics. Even his predecessor, Bodin, who published his famous book in 1576 and was an extreme advocate of the claims of the sovereign, placing him above all law, made him vaguely subject to the Law of God and Nature, and said that he must respect all rights of property and freedom and observe his contracts.

When belief in the Law of Nature died away, the Grotian theory of the sovereign State would at once have spelled anarchy unless some other over-riding authority had been put in its place. So we find some writers limiting the rights of sovereignty by the higher rights of humanity, others by the moral sense of mankind, yet others by the dictates of conscience. The rules imposing limitations upon independence were moral rules, not legal rules. But the sense of civilized communities and the need of intercourse did in effect impose some fetters upon the complete freedom of sovereign States.

Private International Law reconciles the so-called rights of sovereignty where conflict arises : Public International Law partly consists of an endeavour to govern the conflict of the rights of independence. The unfettered independence of a powerful State would otherwise have imperilled the life of all other States. And so gradually there was growing the recognition of a set of rights in other States opposed to the rights of independence. The logic of facts was becoming too much for the crudity of theory.

(a) *Intervention*

The most conspicuous example of the violation of the rights of independence is when one sovereign State intervenes in the affairs of another sovereign State. But intervention is used to cover two very different kinds of action. It is more strictly used when one State intervenes in the internal affairs of another, as for example by action in favour of a particular party in the State. It is also, though less accurately, used to cover the case in which a State interferes in favour of a particular State against other States. In the latter case intervention is the reverse of which independence is the obverse. The discussion of this topic by statesmen and publicists and the endeavours of international lawyers to formulate legal rules to cover it are an admission of the inadequacy of the theory of the sovereign independent State. For if States be fully sovereign and independent, intervention is, as was alleged by " Historicus "[35] in a famous phrase, " a high act of policy above and beyond the domain of law."

Attempts have been made in the past to find a legal justification for intervention on many grounds; most of them have been eventually rejected as insufficient by something approaching the general opinion of publicists. Intervention has, for example, been often justified on the ground of the necessity of maintaining

[35] Sir W. Harcourt, *Letters on Some Questions of International Law*, i.

the Balance of Power[36]—a principle enshrined in the Treaty of Utrecht after the War of the Spanish Succession. It has been justified on the grounds of humanity, as, for example, for the purpose of protecting the Armenian from the brutalities of the Turk. In neither case has the opinion of publicists approved the claim. But in spite of the difficulty in finding a firm juridical foundation for intervention, writers have generally admitted that intervention is justified if it be undertaken for the purpose of self-preservation from a direct, immediate, and serious danger.

Other writers, more advanced, extended the justification of intervention to cases in which the preservation of the social life of the family of nations was threatened. "If a powerful

[36] The motive behind the doctrine of the Balance of Power was the desire to render possible the observance of moral relations in place of the naked exercise of power consequent on an unbalanced aggregation of States. This theory might perhaps be conceived as a forerunner of a League of Nations—the two equipoised leagues rendering possible as long as the balance was maintained fair practice as between all the members of the two leagues. The present war has taught us, however, that the doctrine of the balance of power is not a real or permanent solution of the problem presented by international relations.

State," Dr. Lawrence writes,[37] " frequently endeavours to impose its will on others, and becomes an arrogant dictator when it ought to be content with a fair share of influence and leadership, those who find their remonstrances disregarded and their rights ignored perform a valuable service to the whole community when they resort to force in order to reduce the aggressor to its proper position." States may appoint themselves as special constables. We may interfere to prevent the burglar from pillaging another's house no less than our own. On some such grounds as this the actions of the European Concert were explained—although it was the small offender that the Concert restrained.

Intervention in the internal affairs of another State has also frequently been justified in the past on grounds since held to be wholly insufficient. Sometimes for the purpose of securing dynastic succession, sometimes for the purpose of maintaining a particular system of government. It was with the latter object that the

[37] *Principles of International Law*, p. 133. *Cf.* Westlake, *International Law: Peace*, ch. 13, p. 317.

Holy Alliance was formed; it was because the English government of the day disapproved of that object that they held aloof from that alliance.

In two cases it has however been held justifiable. First, when a government attacks the peace, external or internal, of foreign countries, or when its avowed policy amounts to such a threat. On this ground the Great Powers justly excluded Napoleon from the throne of France.[38] Secondly, " when a country has fallen into such a condition of anarchy as unavoidably to disturb the peace, external or internal, of its neighbours, whatever the conduct or policy of its government may be in that respect."[39] The Entente intervention in Russia can be justified under this head.[40]

The right of intervention in the internal affairs of another State, so far as it is admissible, qualifies in particular the fourth of the rights of independence—the right of a State to

[38] By a Convention of 20th November, 1815.

[39] Westlake, *op. cit.*, ch. 13, p. 318.

[40] Mr. Asquith however on 27th September, 1918, justified the intervention in Russia, first, as an intervention to end an intervention, secondly, as an intervention on humanitarian grounds to prevent cruelty and tyranny.

5

determine its own form of government. The right of intervention in external affairs puts a practical limitation upon all the rights of sovereignty.

(b) *Other Modifications*

There are in addition special limitations upon each of the rights which we have spoken of as attaching to independence.

Even the right of self-preservation is not absolute. Civilized States do not claim the right to kill their prisoners even when there is a shortage of food for their own armies; nor do they claim the right to screen their troops from the enemy fire with women and children. When they do these things, they deny the fact, not the illegality. The Regulations for War on Land made at the Hague in 1907 state expressly that "belligerents do not possess an unlimited right as to the choice of means of injuring the enemy."[41] There are limitations upon the means of destruction that may be employed, upon the right of devastating the enemy's country, and upon the use of deceit

[41] Art. 22.

and treachery. Everyone knows that poisoned arms are not to be used in civilized warfare, and that assassination is not a legitimate method of inflicting injury upon the enemy's cause.

Westlake, one of the greatest of English international lawyers, went even further: for he stated that the right of self-preservation " does not permit us to ward off danger from ourselves by transfering it to an innocent person."[42] A single negative example invalidates a definition. If it be true that a State may not safeguard its State-existence at the expense of a third State, it is not true to say without qualification that a State has an absolute right of self-preservation.

And, indeed, to admit the unlimited right of self-preservation, as do the Germans and too many writers of other nationalities,[43] is to strike at the roots of law between nations. In the cradle of legal beginnings we find the State inducing the victims of wrong to submit their

[42] *Chapters on International Law,* ch. 8; *International Law: Peace,* ch. 13, p. 310.
[43] E.g., Rivier, *Principes du Droit des Gens,* vol. i., Bk. iv., ch. 1, § 19, p. 256.

grievances to the arbitrament of the State; it is not until self-redress is strictly limited within the bounds set for it by the State, and self-defence is itself given a juridical recognition and definition that law can be said to begin. The unlimited right of self-preservation is " the tiger-right " given by the " law " of the jungle and expounded by Huxley with eloquence in his essay on *Natural and Political Rights*.[44] A tiger has the right to do anything to live; he is charged with his own preservation under penalty of death. " Nature, red in tooth and claw with ravin, is the realm of ' tiger-rights.' Her 'laws' are simply statements of cruel facts; her rights are simply brutal powers. To import moral rights of freedom or equality into this sphere is meaningless."[45] For these laws of Nature are the facts which govern the existence of an irrational creation, and something very different from that ideal code—the Law of Nature—into the framework of which Grotius worked his Law of Nations. If we believe that

<hr>

[44] *Method and Results,* pp. 336, sqq.
[45] Ernest Barker, *op. cit.*, p. 134. Compare Hobbes' description of man in a state of nature : *supra,* p. 22.

self-preservation is the ultimate criterion of right and wrong, we are driven to the position of Machiavelli[46] that a " prince cannot observe all those things which are considered good in men, being often obliged, in order to maintain the State, to act against faith, against charity, against humanity, and against religion."

It would seem also that the good sense of the civilized world has imposed some limitations upon the right of sovereign States to exclude foreigners from their territory. It is true that in the arbitration between Great Britain and Belgium over the expulsion of Mr. Ben Tillett from the latter country, M. Desjardins, the arbitrator, held that " the right of a State to exclude from its territory foreigners when their dealings or presence appears to compromise its security, cannot be contested," and that " the State in the plenitude of its sovereignty judges the scope of the acts which lead to this prohibition."[47] But that this right can be involved only if the foreigner is considered dangerous to public order or for con-

---

46 *loc. cit.*
47 *Parliamentary Papers,* 1899, No. 46.

siderations of a high political character was found by the umpire in the later case of Paquet before the Belgian-Venezuelan Mixed Claims Commission 1903.[48]

The right of territorial inviolability (which is better but is not usually treated as a right of sovereignty rather than of independence) in one State is subordinate to the right of self-preservation in another State. So in 1838 when a body of Canadian insurgents moored the *Caroline* on the United States' shore of the Niagara with a view to an attack upon Canada it is generally agreed that the British were justified in crossing over to the New York shore, and sending the *Caroline* adrift down the falls of Niagara. It was only necessary for the British government to show that in self-defence the necessity for the act was instant and overwhelming and left no choice of means.

On analogous grounds the seizure of the Danish fleet by Great Britain in 1807 in order to forestall its falling into the hands of Napoleon and Alexander may well be justified,

[48] *Venezuelan Arbitration of 1903* by J. H. Ralston, pp. 267-8.

although Continental writers are unfortunately in the habit of condemning the British action in this case.

Some jurists of repute speak of a right of peaceful passage over another State's territory or of a right inherent in a State which possesses only the upper reaches of a navigable river to navigate the lower reaches. It may be doubted whether the moral claim of the upper riparian owner to such right of passage can yet be called a right, but there is no doubt that international practice and opinion are alike tending in the direction of the creation of such a right. (Compare President Wilson *infra* p. 145).

(c) *The Effect of Treaties*

But, indeed, if, as most publicists do, we attach a binding force to treaties, that which we have numbered the seventh of the rights of independence—the right of the State to make treaties or alliances with whom it will—imposes a qualification of almost unlimited application upon the other so-called rights. France limited her right of self-defence when by Article 9 of the Treaty of Utrecht she engaged to de

molish the fortifications and to fill up the fort
of Dunkirk, and remained bound by these provisions (which were substantially renewed in
the Treaty of Aix-la-Chapelle in 1748) until the
Treaty of Versailles in 1783.   Prussia limited
her right of self-defence when in 1808 she
gave an undertaking to Napoleon not to maintain in arms more than 42,000 men.   Neither
of these provisions proved to be of long endur-
ance; neither was a success; but neither was
deemed to destroy the sovereignty or independence of the State which entered into the self-
denying engagement.   So, also, difficult as it
is to formulate a legal principle for the justification of intervention on other grounds, there
is no difficulty where the right to intervene is
given by treaty or convention."   Intervention,
then, is for once not " a high act of policy above
and beyond the domain of law," but an act under
the law.   For a voluntary derogation from
sovereignty is not held to impair sovereignty.

---

[19] Phillimore (*On International Law*, vol. i., § 399) however
(followed by Halleck, *International Law*, cc. 4 and 16, vol. i.,
pp. 106, 562) holds the amazing view that wars of intervention
must be justified or condemned without reference to treaty obligations; for, if wrong in themselves, the stipulations of a treaty
cannot make them right.

Belgium was a party to the treaty by which she was neutralized; although by that act her power and her freedom to make war were strictly limited, yet, because she was a party herself to the limitations imposed upon her, she was expressly recognized in the Treaty and has since always been recognized in practice as an independent member of the family of nations.[50]

Again, every State that enters into a treaty of alliance with another State to a greater or less degree surrenders its freedom of action in a sphere where freedom of action would but for such alliance be essential to its independence. The Powers which attended the Hague Conferences did not cease to be independent when they ratified Treaties which imposed additional restrictions upon themselves in limiting the means they might use in war to reduce their enemies to submission.

[50] It may be otherwise in the case of the Grand Duchy of Luxemburg, which was not a party to its own neutralization. (Oakes and Mowat, *Great European Treaties of the Nineteenth Century*, ch. 9). In September, 1918, a demand arose in the Grand Duchy for the revision of the Constitution, embodying a claim for the adoption in the Constitution of the principle that all powers emanate from the nation. The local lawyers were hostile to any proclamation of the sovereignty of the people on the ground that Luxemburg was not neutral by the will of the people but by the will of the European Powers. See *The Law Times*, vol. 145, p. 367.

Stated in another way, we may say that all the other rights of independence must be read as subject to this right.

§7.   THE MEANING OF EQUALITY

It is clear, then, that independence no less than sovereignty does not bear quite its face-meaning for the international lawyer.   It is now desirable to fathom, if possible, the meaning which he attaches to equality.   For sovereign independent States are also equal States.   "In the whole range of the matter discussed in Public International Law," wrote Chancellor Kent[51] in 1826, "no proposition has been more explicitly announced or more implicitly accepted than this: that nations are equal in respect to each other, and entitled to claim equal consideration for their rights, what-ever their relative dimensions or strength may be, or however they may differ in Government, religion, or manners."

Yet in what did that equality consist?   Not in political power; for, even before the Euro-

---

[51] *Commentaries on International Law* (Abdy's edition), ch. 2, p. 46.

pean Concert became a recognized phenomenon in European politics or the Great Powers co-operated for the arrangement of the destinies of the smaller powers, it was clear that a weak power could not deal on equal terms with a strong. Treaties made under duress are no less binding than those made in free consent: else no treaty made at the conclusion of a victorious war would have any legal significance. Not in legislative power; for though the smaller States may in a very real sense be said to have done much to help the growth of International Law—the Germans indeed speak scornfully of it as the creation of weak states,—the content of that law has been given by the great States. Sea-law is made by the practice of the great maritime powers; the laws of war are the rules which the great military powers have laid down for the guidance of their armies, and which those armies have observed in the field.

It has been claimed that modern International Law sprang fully developed from the brain of a Dutchman; Belgians and Swiss, Brazilians and Argentines, have made valuable contributions to the development of the science, but they have had to build that science in accordance with the facts presented to them by the conduct and practice of England and France, Prussia and Russia, Austria and the United States.

Vattel, the great Swiss jurist, in discussing equality said :[52] " A dwarf is as much of a man as a giant; a small republic is no less a sovereign State than the most powerful kingdom." Thus far we can agree; for, in fine, the equality of States amounts to no more than this—that each sovereign independent State is equally entitled to be called a separate State.[53] It does not mean that each State is equal to every other.

The doctrine of the equality of States came from the application by Grotius to International Law of the principles of Roman Law. States were held by Grotius to be in "a state of nature." It followed that States being in their dealings with other States "in a state of nature" could not plead privilege of rank or caste. Similarly, when individual litigants at Rome were " in a state of nature", that is, when they were

---

[52] *Droit des Gens*, Prélim, § 18.
[53] So Westlake says (*International Law: Peace*, ch. 13, p. 321) that " the equality of sovereign States is merely their independence under a different name."

members of a different political community, the particular laws of their own community as to rank or class did not apply, and they were therefore regarded as equal.

§8.   THE "RIGHTS" OF EQUALITY

In order to ascertain the practical conclusions drawn from this theory, I shall pursue the method I have already followed in an endeavour to fix the meaning of sovereignty and independence, and examine the rights which are supposed to flow from the generally admitted equality of States.

These rights are confined to matters of ceremonial.   The chief is the right to send public ministers to any other sovereign State with whom the maintenance of relations of peace and amity is desired.

But this generally admitted equality is evidenced in other ways: every State is entitled to make use of its own language in treaties with another State; and so punctilious was the regard for equality amongst the parties to the Treaty of Vienna that the signatures thereto were appended in alphabetical order.   Hence arose also the practice of the *alternat*—a diplomatic device by which the signatures to treaties are in a different order in different copies. Each sovereign State has the right to regulate the maritime ceremonial to be observed within its own jurisdiction, and where the extent of that jurisdiction has been in dispute maritime ceremonials have often been made the pretext of war. In 1877 the maritime powers agreed to certain international rules to give effect to the principle that all sovereign States with respect to salutes are equal.

§9. MODIFICATION OF THE "RIGHTS" OF EQUALITY

In discussing the rights of equality we have seen that they are for the most part illusory. Even such as they are they may be modified by the consent implied from constant usage or by the express voluntary agreement of one State with another. So the Catholic Powers give precedence to the Pope. Royal States had by usage precedence over Republics, and Emperors used to be reckoned as of more account than Kings. If equality was the rule it was surely only because a number of exceptions prove the rule !

The old text-books on International Law devote a large space to the consideration of questions of ceremonial; for questions of precedence loomed large on the diplomatic horizon. An amusing passage in Macaulay's *History of England*[54] gives an account of the contentions for pride of place between the plenipotentiaries at the Congress of Ryswick. '' The chief business of Harlay and Kaunitz was to watch each other's legs. Neither of them thought it consistent with the dignity of the Crown which he served to advance towards the other faster than the other advanced towards him. If, therefore, one of them perceived that he had inadvertently stepped forward too quick, he went back to the door and the stately minuet began again.'' And history records many other like happenings.[55]

So William Penn, the Quaker, when in 1693 he laid before the world his scheme for

[54] Ch. 22 (Popular edition, p. 624).
[55] See also the entertaining fourth chapter in Sir Ernest Satow's *Guide to Diplomatic Practice.*

a League of Nations, dared not omit[56] some
provision for the susceptibilities of equal sovereigns.   He suggested that in the place of ses-
sion of the Imperial Diet of Europe " to avoid
quarrel for precedency, the room may be round,
and have divers doors to come in and go out
at, to prevent exceptions."

§ 10.   THE MEANING OF " RIGHTS "

These then are the rights which jurists assert
flow from the sovereignty, the independence,
and the equality of States.   There is an old
maxim, *Ubi jus ibi remedium:* there is no
right without a remedy; or as Coke quaintly
said: " Want of remedy and want of right is all
one."[57]   What remedy, then, does International Law provide for the violation of these
rights?   There is diplomatic protest; and, if
that fail, there is war.   But war is a " remedy "
which is open to the evil-doer as well as to the
injured party.   Recourse may be had to war
independently of right and wrong.   The scales
of war are not weighted on the side of justice.

[56] *The Present and Future Peace of Europe,* § 8.
[57] Coke *on* Littleton, 95 b.

Grotius[58] demanded of neutrals that "they should do nothing by which the upholder of a wicked cause might become stronger or by which the movements of a just belligerent might be hampered." Christian Wolff, in 1749, went further.[59] He and his followers held that it was the duty of States to support that power whose war was just. Had the theories of Grotius or Wolff determined the practice of neutral States, war might have acquired something of the character of a legal remedy. But practice did not follow precept. Neutrality tended ever more to predicate complete indifference and an entire aloofness from the moral issues raised between two belligerents. The reason is not far to seek. Every country that goes to war claims that justice is on its side, and in the absence of an objective test which is independent of opinion and makes it unnecessary nicely to balance the right and wrong of a complicated series of facts,[60] who is to decide

[58] *Ubi supra*, iii., 17, 3.

[59] *De Jure Belli Gentium*, ch. 6, §§ 656, 674.

[60] Such an objective test is provided by schemes for a League of Nations; for if one State commences hostilities against another State without submitting the question to arbitration or to the Council of Conciliation the question of "justice" is *ipso facto* determined.

6

with whom the justice lies?   But, though easily explained, the modern conception of neutrality is a terrible indictment of modern civilization; it has been not altogether unjustly said that "a proclamation of neutrality is an announcement by the State which makes it of its determination to let ill alone."[61]

Since, then, in the last resort it has been left to the "irrational and doubtful decision of war," as Erasmus called it,[62] to vindicate the sovereignty, the independence, and the equality of States, and since the scales of war are weighted heavily on the side of the powerful States, sovereignty, independence, and equality, even in the limited sense given to those words by international lawyers, find a place only in the textbooks and not in the practice of Europe. As the present Attorney-General, Sir F. E. Smith, well said, whilst he was still a young man, "In the rough and ready practice of nations suit *in*

---

[61] Lorimer, *op. cit.*, vol. ii., p. 122. Lorimer's book has long suffered from an undeserved neglect. For years the two handsome volumes have been obtainable as a " remainder " for the ridiculous sum of 3s. 6d. If a League of Nations be formed it is possible—in spite of his belief in the Law of Nature—that the stone which the builders rejected will become the head of the corner.

[62] *Complaint of Peace* (English translation (1917), p. 54).

forma pauperis is not a hopeful procedure."[63] The rights of sovereignty, independence, and equality, were moral rights, not legal rights— rights without a remedy; from which fact Lasson draws a characteristically German conclusion: "If things on earth are to be made better, it will be necessary in the first place to rid international relations of the hypocritical phrase of right and of the sacredness of treaties."[64] And perhaps he is right if German policy remains unchanged.

[63] *International Law* (1900), p. 34; (1918), p. 65.
[64] *Princip und Zukunft des Völkerrechts,* p. 15.

III. THE LEAGUE OF NATIONS

WE will now pass from an examination of the position as it is to-day to a contemplation of the possible position after the war. We can only appreciate the extent of the changes involved in this respect in the creation of a League of Nations if we consider how far the world has already departed from the full implications of the theory of the sovereign independent State, how far the modifications of the " rights " have deprived the " rights " of any real substance. If we do this, we shall see just how big a step the governments of the sovereign independent States are asked to take in the hope of thereby enthroning public right in the place now occupied by public anarchy.

§1. SOVEREIGNTY

And first as to sovereignty. We have seen that according to the theory of sovereignty the sovereign has an exclusive power of legislation for his own dominions. But a development of comparatively recent growth has an interesting bearing on this doctrine.

The International Unions, of which there are 12 (e.g., the Telegraph Union, the Postal Union, the Office of Health), constituted at various dates between 1868 and 1907, were almost imperceptibly beginning to exercise a compelling force in their own sphere over the freedom of action of sovereign States. In these Unions the sovereignty of the member State is left untouched; a minority can resist a majority, for unanimity is necessary to make a decision of the Union binding; no rule adopted by the Union is binding on the citizens of any State until ratified by that State, and the State is left to introduce its own legislation to give effect to the rules; disputes on international administration can be submitted to the international bureaux and from them can be referred to arbitration, but the Union has no powers to enforce its decisions; the members of the Union are generally free to leave the

Union. Yet it is impossible in practice for the State to ignore the authority of the Union, and Dr. Bisschop goes so far as to say[1] that these conventions have "undoubtedly created a restriction of the sovereign powers of each member." In the case of most of the Unions that statement might be challenged, but in the case of the International Sugar Union of 1902 it would seem that a real restriction was imposed upon the sovereign powers of the members; for the Union was empowered to take final executory decisions without right of appeal.[2] Such things go to justify the remark of an acute and independent thinker[3] that "governments, if they are not continually reminded of their sacred sovereignty, tend to act as though it mattered very little."

In England and America we may observe another illuminating fact—the recognition given to International Law in the municipal courts. That recognition has been deemed

---

[1] In *Problems of the War* (Grotius Society, vol. ii., p. 127.

[2] See N. Politis in the *Revue de Science et de Législation Financières*: Jan., Feb., March, 1904.

[3] C. Delisle Burns, *The World of States*, ch. 6, p. 94.

to be consistent with the undiminished sovereignty of the State.

When Lord Talbot and Lord Mansfield declared that " the Law of Nations in its full extent was part of the Law of England "[4] they did not mean that England was not a sovereign State. Sir William Scott, afterwards Lord Stowell, sitting in the Prize Court, with ripe and lofty eloquence, said : " I trust it has not escaped my recollection for one moment what it is that the duty of my station calls for from me; namely to consider myself as stationed here, not to deliver occasional and shifting opinions to serve present purposes of particular national interest, but to administer with indifference that justice which the law of nations holds out without distinction to independent States, some happening to be neutral and some to be belligerent. The seat of judicial authority is indeed locally here, in the belligerent country, according to the known law and practice of nations : but the law itself has no locality. It is the duty of the person who sits

---

[4] *Triquet v. Bath*, 4 Burr. 2016.

here to determine this question exactly as he
would determine the same question if sitting
at Stockholm."[5]   Lord Stowell was not sound-
ing the knell of England as a sovereign State.
Nor was the late Lord Parker writing her
epitaph when he gave judgment in the case of
the *Zamora*[6]—a judgment which did much to
establish the confidence of neutrals in the justice
of the British Prize Courts during the present
war.   Lord Parker reaffirmed Lord Stowell's
pronouncement; the law which the Prize Court
administers is not national but international
law;[7] for in a Prize Court "rights based on
sovereignty are waived": "A Court which
administers international law must ascertain
and give effect to a law which is not laid down
by any particular State, but originates in the
practice and usage long observed by civilized
nations in their relations towards each other or
in express international agreement."   In the
same way in municipal Courts in disputes be-

---

[5] *The Maria*, 1 Rob. 340.
[6] 1916, 2 A.C. 91
[7] It is otherwise in Continental Prize Courts : see Sir Francis
Pigott's article in *Problems of the War* (Grotius Society), vol. iii.,
pp. 111, sqq.

tween citizen and citizen recognition is given to the legal effect of custom, although custom is not laid down by the sovereign power.

In the United States the constitution itself by Section 8 of Article 1 gives Congress the power to punish offences against the law of nations, and the judges have as in England treated international law as part of the common law of the land.[8]

For England and America at any rate it would be no great stride to advance from a position in which the rights of sovereignty are implicitly waived in favour of a usage which England may have had no part in creating to an express waiver in favour of laws made by a body on which England had her proper representation. It is true that the implied waiver may be revoked: if the King in Parliament were to make an Act contrary to international law the Courts would enforce the Act and not

[8] For a more precise account of this matter see Picciotto's *Relation of International Law to the Law of England and the United States.* Mr. Picciotto's book was written however before the judgments in the Prize Court and the Privy Council in the case of the *Zamora* were delivered. He has probably therefore slightly modified some of the views expressed in his careful survey of a difficult question.

international law. But there are few English-
men who would wish such an Act passed into
law and it is improbable that any House of
Commons would commit such a moral blunder.
The loss therefore of this power of revocation
by converting an implied into an explicit waiver
would seem to be a formal rather than a real
change.

But in fact no recognized scheme for a
League of Nations makes any such demand
upon the self-abnegation of the sovereign
State. The most extreme suggestion is that
of the American League to Enforce Peace that
conferences between the signatory Powers shall
be held from time to time to formulate and
codify rules of International Law which unless
some signatory shall signify its dissent within
a stated period shall thereafter govern in the
decisions of the arbitral tribunal set up under
the League. Even the scheme of the Fabian
Society only makes the rules proposed by
the International Council binding if ratified.
Clearly in this there is nothing to disturb the
tenderest susceptibilities of the Continental
nations.

But not only has the sovereign State exclusive legislative but also exclusive judicial powers within its own dominions, and over all acts done therein.

"The sovereign," says Grotius,[9] "is one whose acts are not under the power of any other in the sense that they can be rendered void by the decision of any other human will." The German Lasson with most other Germans goes further. "A State," he says,[10] "can never submit to a judicial decision." The world has not accepted this view, but it has been generally agreed that the scope of arbitration excludes questions involving "national independence, vital interests, and national honour." Arbitration treaties in the past have always specifically excluded these questions, and yet have given no definition of what are the questions that involve "national independence, vital interests or national honour." The terms are vague,[11] and almost any international dispute by a State which so wished could be held to involve one

[9] *loc. cit.*, 1, 3, 7.
[10] *Princip und Zukunft des Völkerrechts*, p. 23.
[11] *Cf.* Westlake, *International Arbitration* in *International Journal of Ethics*, October, 1896.

or other of the non-justiciable trinity.   Fortunately States do not in modern times usually wish recourse to war when a settlement can be arrived at in some other way.   During the nineteenth and twentieth centuries many questions which might have been held to fall within the ground forbidden to arbitration have been peacefully and satisfactorily settled by that means.   The delimitation of territorial boundaries may certainly involve "vital interests," yet almost the whole frontier between America and Canada has been settled as a result of a long series of decisions of Courts of Arbitration.   The British Government at first refused to submit to arbitration the claims made by the United States for losses caused to the North in the American Civil War by the fitting out of the *Alabama* and other privateers within the British jurisdiction, on the ground that " Her Majesty's government are the sole guardians of their own honour," yet they eventually changed their mind, and, although the award went overwhelmingly against us, we abode loyally by the result.[12]   Cases such as these

---

[12] Morris, *International Arbitration and Procedure*, ch. 3.

clearly involved the sovereignty of the arbitrating States, yet neither the British nor the American Governments were deemed to derogate from their sovereignty or independence by determining their disputes by the decision of a Court instead of by force of arms.

Since 1914 the United States has entered into Peace Commission Treaties with some thirty other powers, including Great Britain,[13] France, Italy and Russia, but not, significantly enough, Germany, Austria, Turkey, or Bulgaria. The A.B.C. Powers (Argentina, Brazil and Chili) have made a similar treaty. These treaties mark a big step forward in international practice. The parties agree for a period, usually of five years, that all disputes between them of every nature whatsoever, other than those covered by existing arbitration treaties, shall be referred for investigation and report to a Permanent International Commission, and agree not to declare war or begin hostilities during the investigation or before the report is submitted. The report is to be completed

[13] The treaty with Great Britain is easily accessible in Carl Heath's *The Pacific Settlement of International Disputes*, ch. 5.

within a year after the investigation is begun, and after the report has been submitted the parties reserve the right to act independently on the subject-matter of the dispute. Since existing arbitration treaties cover only such justiciable disputes as do not affect vital interests, national independence, and honour, it will be seen that two main classes of dispute fall to be submitted to the Peace Commission : (1) justiciable disputes affecting vital interests, national independence, and honour; (2) non-justiciable disputes.

It may be pointed out that whilst these treaties hold out great hopes for the future of international relations, they implicitly retain the traditional unreal distinction between disputes involving national independence, vital interests, and national honour and those that do not. The true distinction which should be drawn is between disputes susceptible of judicial decision, that is, those arising out of questions as to International Law or the interpretation of treaties and those not susceptible of judicial decision, that is, those not so arising.

In the cases of arbitration above referred to as in the past having successfully found a solution for international difficulties the agreement for arbitration was made *ad hoc*. Under a League of Nations the treaty will bind all the signatories to submit justiciable disputes to a judicial tribunal, and to carry into effect the decisions of that tribunal. The derogation from sovereignty is therefore general. A State so long as it remains a member of the League no longer has a choice whether by a fresh act of its own it shall or shall not submit a particular question for judicial decision. The German delegate at the Hague Conference of 1907, Marschall von Bieberstein, stated[14] that to agree to submit a difference which has arisen to arbitration on terms and before an arbitrator mutually agreed upon was one thing, to be obliged whatever the circumstances to place oneself in the hands of judges not of one's own choosing was something very different. And

[14] *Cf. Parliamentary Papers: Misc.*, No. 4 (1908), pp. 284, 354, 359, 362. So Sir Walter Phillimore: " One of the defects of all arbitration treaties up to now is that they have been not agreements to refer, but agreements to agree to refer, which is a very different thing " (July 23rd, 1917).

indeed it is something very different from the habit of German thought, but not so different from English thought and practice as might be imagined.

To the Germans it is "impossible to conceive"[15] that there should be a judge of a sovereign State not of its own choosing; by a parity of reasoning the sovereign State cannot be bound by law not of its own making. "This truth is unquestionable," says Seydel,[16] "there is no law without a sovereign, above the sovereign, or besides the sovereign; law exists only through the sovereign." The Frenchman, L. Duguit,[17] with a touch of perhaps unnecessary scepticism, says on the other hand, "if there is such a thing as sovereignty of the State it is juridically limited by the rule of Law."

English common sense, as we have seen, has determined that the rule of law is consistent with the retention by the State of its sovereign powers. In the same way it is to be hoped that the common sense of the coming generation

[15] Treitschke : *Politik*, i., 73.
[16] *Grundzüge einer Allgemeinen Staatslehre*, p. 14.
[17] *L'Etat: le Droit Objectif et la Loi Positive*, ch. i. (American translation), p. 247.

will recognize that a general agreement for the submission of questions of legal right and wrong to an impartial tribunal involves no pernicious limitation upon the sovereign right of the State.

There is indeed another difference not yet mentioned between previous international arbitrations and those which would take place within a League of Nations. Hitherto it has been left to the honour of the States concerned to abide by and fulfil the judgments. It is to the credit of the States concerned that, so far as I am aware, every judgment of an arbitral court has in modern times been performed. In a League of Nations, according to almost every plan put forward, the award will have behind it the sanction of the armed force of all the members of the League. To those who believe in the binding force of treaties the addition of a sanction does not add a more serious restriction upon sovereign power than that already admitted.

It must be clearly understood that no scheme yet put forward for a League of Nations

provides an executive for the League.[18]　The
League acts through the States.　The importance of this distinction cannot escape any
reader of the controversies which raged over
the Federal Constitution of the United States.
Alexander Hamilton made it a cardinal point
in his campaign for the substitution of a Federal Government in place of the then existing
Confederation that the Government should
" carry its agency to the persons of the citizens."
" It must," he said, " stand in need of no inter-
mediate legislations; but must itself be empowered to employ the arm of the ordinary
magistrate to execute its own resolutions. . . .
[It] must be able to address itself immediately
to the hopes and fears of individuals.　It must,
in short, possess all the means, and have a right

---

[18] This is not true of individual writers, e.g., Brailsford, and,
tentatively, Lowes Dickinson (*The Choice Before Us*, pp. 193, 209).
Since the MS. of this book was written, however, Viscount Grey,
to whom the progress of the ideals of the League of Nations
movement is due more than any other statesman except President
Wilson, has lent his authority to the proposal for the creation of
an international force.　See below, p. 173.

Every scheme, of course, involves a small secretariat and a
certain unity of command and control.　But it would not be
proper to speak of the present alliance as having an executive
because unity of strategic command has been achieved under
Marshal Foch and economic and financial co-operation under the
various Commissions which have been constituted.

to resort to all the methods, of executing the powers with which it is entrusted, that are possessed and exercised by the governments of the particular States."[19]   No such governmental powers will be accorded to the League of Nations as at present proposed.

In one minor respect it is possible that the formation of a League of Nations may restore rights of sovereignty now lost.   If President Wilson's schemes for securing "the freedom of the seas" are accepted, in a war not waged by the League itself, neutrals will not be subject to some of those infringements of their sovereignty, such as the rules as to contraband and blockade, to which at present they must perforce submit.

We may at this point consider how the theorists on sovereignty would have regarded it in relation to the proposed League.   Would Austin have considered that the sovereignty of the member States was impaired by joining the League?   We shall best be able to answer this question if we examine what Austin's views

[19] *The Federalist*, No. 16,

were on sovereignty in relation to Confederations.

He first distinguishes a Confederation from a Federal State. In a Federal State he holds[20] each of the several States has relinquished a portion of its sovereignty, and consequently the several governments of the several united Societies are jointly sovereign in each and all— the sovereignty resides in the united governments *as forming one aggregate body*. In a system of Confederated States, on the other hand, each of the several Societies is an independent political Society and each of their several governments is properly sovereign or supreme. For neither the terms of the compact framing the Confederation nor the subsequent resolution of the Confederation are enforced in any of the Societies by that aggregate body—they owe their legal effect in each several Society to the authority of that Society. "In short, a system of confederated States is not essentially different from a number of independent governments connected by an ordinary alliance." In the same way, the Frenchman

---

[20] *loc. cit.,* Lect. 6.

Ortolan, states[21] that each of the several States preserves its political identity and its own sovereignty, subject to the restrictions to which it has consented, although it is bound, so far as it is concerned, to give effect to the decisions of the Confederation since it has been a party to the taking of them.

Austin next endeavours to distinguish precisely between confederated States and an alliance. But he " can only affirm generally and vaguely, that the compact of the former is intended to be permanent, whilst the alliance of the latter is commonly intended to be temporary; and that the ends or purposes which are embraced by the compact are commonly more numerous, and are commonly more complicated, than those which the alliance contemplates."[22]

Would Austin then have considered that the League of Nations created a Federal System or a system of confederated States or merely an alliance? No League of Nations likely to be constituted in the near future can fall within

---

[21] *Diplomatie de la Mer* (4th ed.), Bk. i., ch. 2, p. 14.
[22] Austin, *loc. cit.*, p. 269.

Austin's conception of a federal State; we are still far from that " Federation of the World " of which Tennyson had a vision as the goal of human progress. It is more difficult to say whether Austin would have classed the League as a confederation or as an alliance. This may be best considered in the light of a concrete example.

Austin took as an instance of a system of confederated States the German Confederation as it existed between 1820 and 1866.[23] If we examine its constitution we shall at first be struck by the resemblance of some of the provisions to those which occur in the Draft Treaties for a League of Nations. The several States retained the right of entering into relations with foreign States provided they did nothing against the security of any other member or of the Confederation itself. The several States sent plenipotentiaries to a Diet which acted as the organ of the Confederation for common external purposes. It could declare war against foreign States on the territory

[23] The German Confederation of 1820 was unaggressive : it kept the peace. Phillimore, *Three Centuries of Treaties of Peace*, ch. 3, p. 37.

of the Confederation being threatened.   The
Diet had no forces other than those of the several States which it could employ.   It had no
sovereignty over the individual subjects of the
member States; those subjects owed allegiance
to the State government alone.   But, if we look
for differences instead of resemblances, we shall
find these no less noteworthy.   Whilst in the
schemes for a League of Nations a right is generally left to the States to resort to hostilities
against each other in the case of non-justiciable
disputes, provided the procedure for a *moratorium* is first complied with, in the German Confederation the States were not allowed to make
war on each other in any circumstances.   Further, the Confederated States mutually guaranteed each other's possessions.   The Diet,
moreover, could receive and accredit envoys
and conclude treaties on behalf of the Confederation.   These distinctions seem to suggest that
a League of Nations would probably have been
classed by Austin as an alliance rather than a
confederation.   · If that be the case, no one
would deny to the several States independence
or sovereignty.   Yet it will be an alliance of

wider scope, of nobler aim and (we may hope) of greater permanence than any which history records.   It will be an alliance showing some of the characteristics of a Confederation.   According to our temperament we shall draw despair or hope from the undoubted historic fact that no Society of confederated States has long survived; the States have either separated and formed new combinations or strengthened their bonds and become a federal union.[24]

Since Austin considered that in a Confederation the sovereignty of the constituent States was unimpaired, to him it would have had no bearing on our present discussion, whether the League was held to be a Confederation or an alliance.   But most modern writers on International Law make a relevant distinction, and hold that, whilst allied States retain their sovereignty and independence in full, confederated States are possessed only of an imperfect independence.

It was a cardinal tenet of the theory of sovereignty as expounded by the earlier writers that sovereignty was in its nature one and indivis-

[24] See Appendix I.

ible. Bodin and Hobbes, Bentham and Austin, differing on much else, all agreed on this.[25] " Theories of sovereignty," it has been said,[26] " have been more often apologies for a cause than the expression of a disinterested love of truth." In no respect is that more true than in respect of the extremely artificial doctrine[27] that sovereignty cannot be divided. It has served the interest of polemics, not of truth.

The uses to which it has been put are various. Hobbes used it as a weapon with which to denounce the Papacy. In the American Civil War the leaders on both sides proclaimed that sovereignty was indivisible. But, whereas the Northerners found that under the constitution the sovereignty was in the nation as a whole, the Southerners, led by Calhoun, held that the sovereignty was left in the separate States. In fact, the American Constitution—Viscount Bryce suggests perhaps intentionally[28]—left the point, which involved the right of the States to secede or determine the Federation, indeter-

---

[25] *Aliter* William Penn, *Op. cit.* Conclusion.
[26] Jethro Brown, *Austinian Theory of Law*, p. 272.
[27] Bryce, *loc. cit.*, p. 93.   [28] *Ibid*, p. 106.

minate.   It was left for a decision to be given *de facto* by the sword.

So long as the question, who is the sovereign, is left open, there is, as Sir Leslie Stephen has said,[29] "a condition of unstable equilibrium or latent anarchy."

Yet we find the same evasion of this important point in the Constitution of the German Confederated States in 1820.   The States had no formally recognized right to withdraw from the Confederation.   From this some writers[30] infer that they had by implication a right to secede, others[31] that they had not.

Still more surprising at first sight in the light of the lessons of the American Civil War is the fact that of the schemes for a League of Nations put forward by the American and English Societies neither gives any indication whether a member of the League is to be allowed to withdraw from it.   Advocates of the League hold widely different views on this point : Mr. Brailsford says that, since the es-

---

[29] *Hobbes,* ch. 4, p. 200.
[30] E.g., Jethro Brown, *op. cit.,* p. 152.
[31] E.g., Hall, *op. cit.,* Pt. i., ch. 1, p. 27.

sence of the League is a voluntary association of nations, " the right of secession from it must be acknowledged and respected."[32] Lord Parker of Waddington on the other hand seems to have believed that most advocates of the League hold the other view: " To admit the right of its members to withdraw from the League," he wrote when pointing out the difficulties in the way of the League, "would be as fatal to the League's sovereign power as would have been the recognition of the right to secede from the Union to the sovereign right of the United States."[33]

It would seem, however, clear that in the beginning the League must be a society of free States, joining the League of their own free will and at liberty to leave it of their own free will, provided sufficient notice is given of their intention so to do. The essence of the Roman law of partnership, *Societas*, was that it was voluntary. It was founded on the free consent of the partners. No one could be made a part-

[32] *A League of Nations*, ch. 10, p. 307.
[33] In a letter to *The Times*, June 25, 1918.

ner against his will. For you cannot rely upon the good faith of a man who is forced into an association against his will. "The Jacobin interpretation of fraternity, 'Be my brother, or I'll kill you,' is not the language of sound statesmanship."[34] But force of circumstances may drive a man irresistibly into a partnership. If the League of Nations is joined by all the great States but one, that one outside will be unable to claim the assistance of the others when in the right, but exposed to the full weight of their joint hostility when deemed to be in the wrong. Such a position would not long be tenable.[35]

But *Societas* was voluntary, not only in its inception but also in its termination. It was a maxim of Roman law that no one can be compelled to remain in a partnership against his will. The idea of fraternity is characteristic of the relation of partnership. In order to safeguard the interests of the remaining partners the rule was introduced that where a partner

---

[34] Sir Roland K. Wilson, *The Province of the State*, ch. 13, p. 224.

[35] *Ibid*, ch. 1, p. 11 ; ch. 13, p. 219.

renounced his partnership with an improper end in view or at a time injurious to the partnership interests he should be penalised. He remained liable to the others to the extent of the loss occasioned to them by his defection; whilst he had no share in any profit made subsequent to the renunciation. So perhaps with the League of Nations. If the Constitution leaves the point open as did that of the United States it is possible that in course of time, as the League extends its activities and gains the confidence of its members, it will come to be recognized that to abandon the League would be an apostasy which, if persisted in, would be so just a cause for suspicion in the abiding members of the League that it would justify recourse to war.

Should that time come, if the theory that sovereignty is one and indivisible be retained, we should probably be driven to concede that, as in America, the States had yielded their Sovereignty to the Union. "Sovereignty," says a popular writer,[36] " is the very essence of

---

[36] F. S. Oliver, *Alexander Hamilton*, Bk. vi., ch. 6,

union." But is sovereignty really indivisible? That is not the view which has approved itself to the Supreme Court of the United States. It seems clear that the legal sovereignty as distinct from the practical sovereignty may for different purposes reside in different organs. The distinction between practical and legal sovereignty has been well explained by Viscount Bryce: practical sovereignty "is the power which receives and can by the strong arm enforce obedience"; legal sovereignty "belongs to him who can command obedience as of right."[37] The weight of modern authority is that internal legal sovereignty is divisible.[38]

If internal sovereignty is not indivisible a breach has been made in the inexpugnable fortress of traditional theory—a theory designed for polemical purposes with a view to internal rather than external sovereignty. If we look at facts rather than theories we shall find examples which seem to prove that *de facto* it has already been recognized that external sovereignty also may be distributed in different organs for different purposes.

[37] *Op. cit.*, p. 69.   [38] E.g., Bryce, Jethro Brown, Oppenheim.

When the Ionian Islands were in 1815 placed as a free and independent State under the protectorate of Great Britain, they retained a separate trading flag, continued to receive consuls, and were not affected by British treaties. But their executive was appointed by Great Britain and they were represented in external relations by Great Britain. Yet in the Crimean War it was held that the State of the Ionian Islands was neutral.

By the Act which provided for the neutrality and autonomous government of the Samoan Islands in 1889 Great Britain, Germany, and the United States agreed that, whilst the Samoans were to be independent and free to elect their Chief or King, should any dispute arise about the election or the powers of the King, it should be decided by reference to the Chief Justice who was to be appointed by one of the three signatory Powers. Any difference between any of those Powers and Samoa was to be decided not by war but by the Chief Justice; who moreover in his criminal jurisdiction was to apply the law of the United States, England, or Germany as he should think most appropriate, and in the case of natives the laws and customs of Samoa."[39] ·

In these two cases (and there are others) we clearly see a division of external sovereignty in fact. If the power of the League grows to such an extent that the right of secession is lost we shall have another instance of the same thing. And this may also prove to be the case if the League having justified itself by success gradually gains in legislative and executive power.

§2. INDEPENDENCE

(a) *Intervention*

The "rights" of independence must be considered in detail. The first thing that will strike us is that the whole character of intervention will be changed in those cases in which a member of the League violates the provisions of the Treaty.

In the past intervention has always raised a moral problem, for there was a clash between the right to independence of the intervening

[39] Professor Simeon E. Baldwin, *The Division of Sovereignty,* in *International Law Notes,* vol. iii., p. 59.

State and the right to independence of the
State in whose affairs it intervened. Under a
League of Nations intervention in fulfilment
of the obligations imposed by the League will
no longer be "an act of high policy" but the
performance of an obligation; it will no longer
be the reverse of which independence is the
obverse, but its complement; neutrality will no
longer be a duty but a crime against the Society
of States. In such cases the right of self-
preservation is reinforced by the duty in the
colleague States of lending their aid for the
preservation of the wronged State. So in the
present war Great Britain is implementing her
obligation to preserve the independence of
Belgium.

(b) *Other Modifications*

(1) The right to self-preservation will be
further limited, for it will no longer be possible
in justification of a sudden attack upon a
neighbour to appeal to the right to prevent and
forestall an imminent attack from him. The
moratorium before recourse is had to war provided by all schemes for a League of Nations

will preclude that possibility. But in the past also, as we have seen,[40] States have voluntarily limited the means employed even to preserve their own being. The period of self-denial which States anxious to go to war will impose upon themselves by joining the League will not be the first voluntary restriction put upon the right of self-preservation.

"Relative disarmament" is sometimes put forward as an essential of a League of Nations. That is not so; and many hope that the two problems will be kept distinct. But even if the members of the League do agree upon a scheme for relative disarmament it will not affect their independence. It has never been suggested that if Great Britain and Germany had come to an agreement at the time of the Haldane mission they would have lost their status as independent States. Armies and navies will still be raised and used only by their own States, although each State may have entered into a binding obligation to use its forces upon the happening of certain events. War will be

[40] Above, p. 50.

declared by the State under an obligation to the League, just as a State may be under an obligation to declare war in pursuance of a treaty of guarantee.[41] Again it is possible that under a League of Nations Turkey might be left independent and yet prohibited from fortifying Constantinople : France did not cease to be independent after the Treaty of Utrecht, nor did Russia in 1856 when she agreed to refrain from establishing military and maritime arsenals on her coast of the Black Sea.

Cardinal Gasparri during the present war proposed that one of the terms of peace should be that conscription should be made illegal in all countries. And the same demand is made by a large number of the advocates for the formation of a League of Nations. It is not however an essential or integral part of the scheme. Should the peace terms include any such provision it would involve a definite voluntary limitation upon the rights arising from the independence of the member States, for it

[41] See Ex-President Taft's paper at the First Annual Assemblage of the League to Enforce Peace, Washington, May 27, 1916, in *Enforced Peace,* p. 59.

has been consistently held that a general diffusion of military science and training is a legitimate means of self-preservation which cannot be called into question by other States.[42]

(2) The vague and indeterminate right of a State to increase its dominions and its power by all lawful means will be given a more definite shape. It is generally suggested that in addition to the Judicial Tribunal a Council shall be constituted for the purposes of inquiry and mediation. It is not, however, generally recognized that inquiry and mediation are in their nature distinct. The object of commissions of inquiry is to suggest what to the Council seems the best solution; the object of mediation is to find the solution (whether intrinsically just or not) which both parties will be prepared to accept. The difference is that between the methods of an industrial arbitrator and those of Sir George Askwith.[43]

It is not generally[44] proposed that the recom-

---

[42] Burlamaqui, *Droit Naturel*, Pt. iv., ch. i., § 13; Halleck, *op. cit.*, vol. i., ch. 4, p. 122.

[43] See Woolf, *The Framework of a Lasting Peace*, p. 37.

[44] Otherwise in the Draft Treaties of the Fabian Society and the Dutch Committee. And see below, p. 143.

mendations of the Council of Conciliation shall have any binding force, although on the analogy of the Peace Commission Treaties hostilities must not be commenced until the Council has reported. No serious limitation will therefore be imposed upon the independence of the signatory States. But the report especially in cases of inquiry as distinct from those of mediation will at least provide some guidance to help determine what means are and what means are not innocent and lawful. The decisions of the Council will not be binding but they will, if the League is a success, have a determinant moral effect, and will very possibly decide the course of action of the other signatory States in any war that may arise.

(3) A League of Nations does not necessarily involve any limitation on the right of a nation to monopolize its own trade. Even if the members of the League, as some of its advocates desire,[45] agreed not to discriminate against each

---

[45] So the greatest of all the advocates, President Wilson, in his speech at New York on 27th September, 1918 : " There can be no special, selfish economic combinations within the League, and no employment of any form of economic boycott or exclusion, except as the power of economic penalty by exclusion from the markets of the world may be vested in the League of Nations itself as a means of discipline and control." See below, pp. 164-6.

other from any motive of political hostility, that would only be an extension of the "most favoured nation" policy which already obtains. And indeed the weight of international opinion was already before the war definitely against any such right of unfair discrimination.

In 1888 Mr. Bayard, Secretary of State for the United States, protested against the imposition upon American citizens of a tax from which the citizens of another power were exempt, and appealed to "the general principle of the law of nations which justifies this government in insisting that there shall be no undue discrimination against citizens of the United States wherever they may be resident."[46] The long controversy between Germany and the U.S.A. with reference to the inspection of American pork exported to Germany ended on paper in a vindication of the same principle. But Germany, though she repealed the decree excluding American pork, in practice still imposed harassing and vexatious difficulties in the way of the importers.[47]

[46] Moore, *Digest of International Law*, ii., 57.
[47] Ellery Stowell, *International Cases*, i., 292-5.

(4) The League will in no way interfere with the right of the member State to choose its rulers or its own form of government. It may however be noted that long ago Montesquieu pointed out[48] that Confederations worked best in the case of republics : it is improbable that any autocracy will be admitted to the League, or that if it were it would long remain a member. The admission of Philip of Macedon as a member destroyed the Amphictyonic Council.

(5) It would not seem that the formation of the League will in any way further curtail the right of a State to exclude foreigners from its territory.

(6) We have seen that relative disarmament is not a necessary or inevitable condition of a League of Nations. If however a satisfactory scheme for relative disarmament can be devised (and it is devoutly to be hoped that it can), then it seems clear that there must be provisions to secure that no faithless member of the League shall secretly exceed the limits

---

[48] *De L'Esprit des Lois*, Bk. ix., ch. 2.

set for its military or naval forces. Those provisions would probably involve a right of visit and inspection in favour either of the officials of the League or of the accredited representatives of any member State. This would set a new limitation upon the right of territorial inviolability.

(7) Implicit or explicit in any scheme for a League of Nations is the provision that no treaty shall be entered into by a member inconsistent with the terms of the treaty constituting the League.[49] But this implies no new limitation upon the right of the sovereign States to negotiate what treaties they will. In the past also sovereign States have restricted their own power to make new treaties by the terms of alliances already formed with other States. This self-imposed restriction has been rightly regarded as affecting only the *exercise* of the power of making treaties, not as a modification of the *power* itself.[50]

---

[49] President Wilson expresses this idea in the following words: "There can be no leagues or alliances or special covenants and understandings within the general and common family of the League of Nations." (Sept. 27, 1918).

[50] Halleck, *Op. cit.*, vol. i., ch. 8, p. 293.

A similar conclusion will be arrived at in connexion with the proposal in The Minimum Programme of the Central Organization for a Durable Peace (whose offices are at The Hague) that all secret treaties shall be void. The open diplomacy demanded by President Wilson[51] involves no real limitation upon the treaty-making power of member States.

(c) *The Effect of Treaties*

It may be hoped that the formation of a League of Nations will give the solution of one of the problems which have most vexed international lawyers. We have seen that according to German theory States are bound by treaties only so long as it is convenient to them to remain bound. In 1908, putting this theory into practice, Ferdinand of Bulgaria issued a declaration of independence, and Francis Joseph of Austria-Hungary annexed Bosnia and Herzegovina in flat violation of the Treaty of Berlin of 1878.

The binding force of treaties had been declared in its most categoric form by the Great

[51] See below, pp. 155, 162. *Cf.* Clause 15 of the Fabian Scheme.

Powers (including Austria-Hungary) in 1870. In 1856 by the Treaty of Paris Russia was prevented from maintaining a fleet in the Black Sea; in 1870, taking advantage of France's pre-occupation with the war with Prussia, she denounced this provision of the Treaty. A conference was held of the Powers signatory to the Treaty of Paris, and the Powers that attended—Great Britain, Germany, Austria-Hungary, Russia, and Turkey —(whilst conceding to Russia what she had taken for herself) made a solemn declaration that "it is an essential principle of the law of nations that no power can liberate itself from the engagements of a treaty, or modify the stipulations thereof, unless with the consent of the contracting powers by means of an amicable arrangement."

Most English writers have chosen the middle course between the stringency of the 1870 declaration and the immoral absolution given to States by Treitschke.[52] Each extreme doctrine flows from following State-independ-

[52] And unfortunately some other writers who are not Germans, e.g., Fiore, *Nouveau Droit International*, Pt. i., ch. 4.

ence to its logical conclusion. If we look at the State which wishes to release itself from its obligation, then, if its independence means that it is above and beyond the law, it may repudiate treaties at its pleasure. So Treitschke.

If we look at the parties who wish to uphold the treaty, then any one of them, if it be a completely independent unit, may hold that State which wishes to be released to the letter of its bond, even though all the other States party to the agreement think it right that it should be released. Unanimity is requisite to the extinction of a treaty. So the Great Powers in 1870.

Neither doctrine is completely satisfactory. The one presents us with anarchy in a world in which reliance upon the faith of the written word is dead; the other is condemned by its rigidity in a world where circumstances are always changing.

So also in the relations of man to man the war has emphasized the fact that the old rule of the Common Law that a man will be held to the performance of that which he has unconditionally undertaken to perform is not all-sufficient. New circumstances the coming of which cannot be foreseen may render it unjust to hold a man to his promise. The perpetuation of the *status quo* when its justification is gone is perhaps the greatest danger of observed treaties. Austria could indefinitely have prevented the unification of Italy. The necessary conjunction of elasticity with strict respect for the pledged word may be found under a League of Nations in one or both of two ways. Cases in which in the opinion of a State circumstances have so changed that a treaty should be abrogated are eminently suitable for reference to the Council of Conciliation. It would be possible also to give to a majority of the signatories to a treaty (not necessarily to a bare majority) the power to release a party from his engagements when circumstances have substantially altered, and in this way to make juridical provision for necessary change.

§3. EQUALITY

In a League of Nations all the States composing it will be equal in a way they were not before—equal before the law. In the vindication of those rights which are given a juridical basis by the League all States will be equal; for before the law, whatever the disparity of power, all claimants are equal in their right and in the remedy to maintain that right. Under the League each suitor will rely not only on his own power but on the power of all his colleagues. The small State will no longer sue *in forma pauperis*. "Law," wrote the German poet Schiller bitterly, "is the friend of the weak."

Whilst equality under the League of Nations will have more reality than it had in 1914, States will still not be in fact equal. Municipal law has to recognize the inequality of individuals—economic inequality, intellectual inequality and so forth. He that can bear the burden must bear the burden, and he that is subject to undue economic pressure must be protected. International Law also must, if the League is to be a success, give recognition to international facts. Montenegro will not, as at the Hague Conferences, have an equal vote with England in determining the laws of naval warfare. A consideration of the British Empire shows the absurdity of "one State one vote." The British Empire whilst it remained strong in union would only have one vote; if it were weakened by the severance of the legal ties which bind Canada, Australia, and South Africa to Great Britain, the same peoples would have four. Representation must be in proportion to power.[53] Municipal law is observed because it is made and it is enforced in accordance with the will of those that have the power. At first the League will have neither strictly legislative nor executive powers. If it ever obtains them, only if the legislative and the executive of the League of Nations answer to and represent the power behind the League, would they achieve their purpose. Legal institutions are ultimately based on power. For law must not transcend the facts, and no legal institution that is not

[53] There are however advocates of a League who do not accept this view. The question of the best machinery to give effect to it is by no means clear. It has been suggested that voting power should be based on a factor derived from a comparison of man power with financial and economic resources and intellectual and moral character. That is too complicated; but it is difficult to find a system of representation which will do justice alike to the British Empire and France, Belgium and Russia,

supported by those who have the power for the time being has any stability.

§4.   RIGHTS

If we ask what changes a League of Nations would make in the alleged rights of the sovereign independent State, we shall at once see that it will give to those rights which are recognized some reality, will transfer them from the text-books to the forum.   It will give a new meaning to the word "rights" in International Law.   Jural relations will more nearly correspond with the actual relations of States in practice.   Even if we cling to the traditional language of the jurist and the publicist, if we still speak of the sovereign, independent, and equal State, those words will have gained a new fullness of meaning, a new body.   For, if the rights are recognized under a League of Nations, they will be enforceable—enforceable by the combined will and power of the whole League. Law follows morality.   We shall have reached the stage when the moral rights governing the relations of States have been converted into legal rights.

§5.   SUMMARY

If for a moment we review the ground which we have traversed, we shall come to the conclusion that the formation of a League of Nations does not necessarily mean any radical alteration in the modified conceptions of sovereignty, independence, and equality, which were the received doctrines of the nineteenth century.   For the nineteenth century recognized[54] that Belgium remained a sovereign independent State in spite of her neutralization, and that the States which guaranteed it remained sovereign independent States in spite of the obligations which they had taken upon themselves.   Once the sovereignty and independence of Belgium are admitted, it is no further step to hold that the State which voluntarily joins a League to keep and enforce the peace, and so voluntarily to that extent surrenders the power of arbitrarily determining its future course of action, remains a sovereign and independent State.

[54] *Cf.* e.g. Lawrence, *uli supra,* § 43, p. 79.   Oppenheim, *International Law,* vol. i., § 97.

How unsubstantial the fabric of these moral rights of sovereignty often was may be seen from the case of Turkey. Since the 16th century by a series of arrangements known as the Capitulations, European powers had withdrawn their nationals in Turkey from the jurisdiction of the Turkish Courts for most criminal and civil purposes, and justice had been done to them in the consular Courts of their own powers. When, in 1856, Turkey was admitted to the family of nations, the Capitulations remained, although one of the State's so-called rights of sovereignty is an exclusive authority over all persons, things, and acts within its territory. Rumania, Serbia, and Japan in the same way have all been subject to Capitulations when sovereign independent States. Still more shadowy was the sovereignty or suzerainty of Turkey in Egypt in recent years. In 1911 it was still officially recognized in spite of the English occupation; but Italy, regarding facts rather than theories, treated Egypt as neutral in the Italo-Turkish War of that year.

Or again consider the case of Cracow. By the Treaty of 1815 Cracow was declared to be

9

independent, and its independence was guaranteed by Austria, Russia, and Prussia. For the following thirty years the Councils of this independent State were habitually influenced by the guaranteeing powers. Yet, when in 1846 Cracow was annexed by Austria, Great Britain, France, and Sweden protested on the ground that the annexation was a violation of the Treaty of 1815. It is a just inference that the fact that Cracow's policy was not its own in the intervening period was not considered as altering its status as an independent State.

The League will, however, provide a sanction for the breach of obligations for which previously there was no sanction and so give States an equality in fact which they have never before possessed. And if the future prove that the League meets a human need and its legislative and executive power is extended, it may well be that we shall have an example of divided sovereignty on an incomparably larger scale than we have ever had before.

IV. THE FREE SELF-GOVERNING STATE

IT is unnecessary, therefore, to go so far as the American Professor who proclaims that "we shall never separate the truth from vitiating error until we have broken utterly with all our traditional doctrines of the State in terms of that plausible philosophical conception, 'sovereignty.'"[1] But why should we cling to this old jargon of the Court-house and the Academy, of the platform and the Chancellories? The use of clear and unambiguous terms is almost essential to clear thinking. One of the greatest gifts of the Greeks to the development of philosophy was the vocabulary with which they endowed it; for the terminology compelled clear thought.

[1] Professor Small, of Chicago, in *Americans and the World Crisis*.

Sovereignty, independence, and equality are vague and misleading words which common people are apt to understand in their primary meaning and statesmen and publicists use in a very different sense. They overlap; sovereignty adds nothing to that which is already given by independence. It is, as another American writer[2] has recently said, "futile to introduce the conception of sovereignty into international law." We owe our modern ideas on sovereignty largely to John Austin, but that master of clear analysis admitted[3] that the difficulty adhering to the phrases "sovereignty" and "independent society" arose "from the vagueness or indefiniteness of the terms in which the definition or rule is inevitably conceived." The nebulous notions of sovereignty and independence have clouded, and not illuminated, the true relations of States in the past. It is no less necessary for legal science to conform to the facts of human relations than it is for grammatical science to conform to the facts of language.

[2] P. A. Brown in *American Journal of International Law*, ix., 326.

[3] *Op. cit.*, p. 236

Huxley,[4] in his declining years looking back upon his life, declared his conviction, which had grown with his growth, and strengthened with his strength, " that there is no alleviation for the sufferings of mankind except veracity of thought and of action, and the resolute facing of the world as it is when the garment of make-believe by which pious hands have hidden its uglier features is stripped off." To those that had eyes to see, the Germans stripped the make-believe from sovereignty and independence; but, instead of shuddering at the horrible immorality of that which was exposed, they gloried in it. It is for us an act of cowardice to turn away our eyes from the truth which has been revealed; we must steadfastly face it, and make it our resolve to abandon the make-believe with which in the past we have allowed ourselves to be deceived and, knowing the evil, to shun it.

Human relations change : International Law is an evolutionary science. The ideas of sovereignty and the rights which attach to it have

---

4 In his *Autobiography*.

changed in the past; there is every reason to believe that in the future also they will be modified.[5] One may still meet here and there a friend who will deplore the decadence of the age because his villagers or his employees do not always touch their cap to him when they meet him. But the spirit of the age recognizes that our friend's real dignity is not thereby impaired. The sense of values has become different. In the not so very distant past one State has engaged another in war because that other had not honoured its flag with the ceremonial it expected, and kings have immolated their peoples for their dynastic purposes. To-day, even in the midst of the most bloody war in all history, war between the Great Powers for such a reason is almost unthinkable.

The object of the State is to secure the greatest amount of freedom possible for its citizens; the object of International Society is the realization of the freedom of separate nations; for freedom is " the perfect relation of all separate rational entities."[6] The ideal attainment of these objects we call Justice.

[5] *Cf.* Jethro Brown, *op. cit.*, p. 273.
[6] Lorimer, *Op. cit.*, vol. i., p. 1.

These are ethical propositions. Law, if it conform to the demands of Justice, gives a practical application to Ethics. Rights are the means given by the Law for the achievement of freedom. Now freedom demands a recognition of the freedom of others: the assertion of the absolute supremacy or independence of one State involves a denial of freedom to every other State. Freedom and absolute independence are irreconcilable. Freedom is at the opposite pole to anarchy. Hence, it has been said,[1] that the unavoidable paradox of State-action is that it uses force to create freedom. In order to attain our own or our neighbour's real and ultimate freedom we may have to encroach upon our own or our neighbour's proximate and apparent freedom. The members of a League of Nations will gain their freedom at the cost of their apparent independence; for freedom can come only under the Law. If a League of Nations achieves its object, it will introduce the reign of Law in place of the reign of Might, and International

[1] Ernest Barker, *op. cit.*, p. 37. *Cf.* Rousseau, *Contrat Social,* i., 7.

Law will represent, no longer an ethical as-
piration, but the actual relations of inter-de-
pendent States. The rights of the State will
be legal rights inherent in it as a member of the
Society which recognizes those rights.

The problem is that presented by Hobbes'
picture of man in the state of nature. The
solution is that found by Rousseau for Hobbes'
problem. The problem is "to find a form of
association, which defends and protects with
all the force of the community the person and
property of each associate, and by which each
one uniting with all obeys only himself, and
remains as free as he was before." The solution
is that "each of us puts in common his person
and all his power under the supreme direction
of the general will; and we receive again each
member as an indivisible part of the whole. . . .
In a word, each giving himself to all gives himself to none; each associate acquires over others
the same right which he yields over himself;
he gains the equivalent of all that he loses, and
with it greater force to keep what he has."[8]

[8] Rousseau, *Contrat Social*, i., 4.

The doctrine of the Social Contract as an account of the historical genesis of the State is palpably false; its logical truth as an explanation of the State in being is not thereby impugned. If a League of Nations or a Society of States is created, the Social Contract will give both the historical and the logical explanation of the new order of international relations.

We shall do well, then, not to lay stress upon the independence of States but upon their interdependence, not upon their external but upon their internal sovereignty. We shall speak not of the sovereign independent State but of the Free Self-Governing State.

If we apply the same test to the conception of the free self-governing State that we have already applied to the sovereign independent State we shall find the key alike to the rights and duties of the State in the Golden Rule— "Whatsoever ye would that men should do to you do ye even so to them; for this is the law and the prophets," and in its negative form, "Do not that unto others which ye would not that they should do unto you." In virtue of its freedom the State will have the right to take all necessary measures to preserve its own corporate life, the right to extend its dominions or influence, the right to control its own trade, the right to decide for itself by whom and in what manner it shall be governed, the right to determine what privileges shall be attached to its citizenship and who shall be admitted to those privileges, and the right to make treaties or conventions with whom it will, provided in each case that its action is consistent with the like rights inherent in other States and with any special engagements by which it is bound to other States. These limitations are imposed by the very nature of freedom; for the freedom of one implies the freedom of all, and the obligatory force of treaties springs from the freedom of the will which consents to their making.

By reason of the fact that it is self-governing the State will have an exclusive authority over all persons, things and acts within its territory; it will make its own laws, and enforce them itself, it will administer its own justice, it will impose its own taxes and apply its revenue as it pleases, it will regulate the life of its own citizens and of all foreigners who may be in its dominions. It will still be able to enforce its own laws against its own citizens who are abroad when they return within its own jurisdiction. The only derogations from its exclusive authority in this regard will be those to which it has freely submitted by any special engagements into which it may have entered with other States. And these, it may be safely conjectured, will be only such as for the conveniency of government and the promotion of justice and morality give a reciprocal recognition of rights created by municipal law. National morality is aided by the recognition of a French marriage as binding in England, and an English marriage as binding in France, and extradition treaties make for the establishment of justice.

V. THE ULTIMATE AIM OF INTER-NATIONAL ORGANIZATION·

A WISE and eloquent writer, Professor Ramsay Muir, has said[1] that whereas "internationalism is dependent upon nationalism . . . internationalism is necessary as the fulfilment of nationalism. The two are as mutually dependent as Liberty and Law." The goal to which history is painfully making its way is the reconciliation of cosmopolitanism with patriotism. The goal will be won when national freedom of action is vindicated, not apart from, but in and through, the recognition of international dependence. Then no longer shall we deem, as Treitschke deemed, the glory of a State to lie in the strength of its egotism, but rather in the loyalty of its co-operation with other States in safeguarding freedom.

---

[1] *Nationalism and Internationalism*, p. 223.

International order will be based on the permanent satisfaction of national aspirations.

The League of Nations will help to this end. At first it can be only a cautious movement in the right direction. War under the schemes put before us is not only a police measure. The State is left at liberty to make war for what it thinks sufficient cause at its own discretion, provided the dispute is not susceptible of judicial decision and provided the point at issue has first been submitted to the good offices of other powers for mediation. But when we think of the capricious nature of the judgments given by War, and of the human loss and suffering involved in the bloody decision of the battlefield, then we feel that soon, if a League be once formed, war will be recognized as justified only when it is used by the common purpose of the Society of Nations to prevent and punish the aggressor against international law and order—

" Oh ! then a longing like despair
    Is to their farthest caverns sent ;
For surely once, they feel, we were
    Parts of a single continent !"

APPENDIX I

THE LEAGUE OF NATIONS AND THE MAKING OF THE AMERICAN CONSTITUTION

I HAVE not attempted in this book to state the case for a League of Nations, to show the need for it or that it will accomplish its purpose. Nor have I attempted to give the *pros* and *cons* of this or that variation in the forms which the League may take. Still less has it been my object to cast doubts upon the end at which it aims or to seek for and expound the difficulties which stand in the way of the realization of its purpose. This short note therefore seems properly relegated to an Appendix.

So far as I can remember, the analogy between the problem now confronting the British,

French, and American Governments and that
which confronted the framers of the Constitution of the United States has not been fully considered.   Yet the difficulties and controversies
of 1918 have many resemblances to those of
1781-1789, which so largely centred round the
question of sovereignty that it would not be
right to omit all reference in this book to that
epoch-making campaign.

A hundred and thirty years ago the proposals
for the loss or diminution of the sovereignty of
the Thirteen States excited a bitterness which
fortunately has so far for the most part been
missing in the discussions on a League of Nations.   The articles of Alexander Hamilton
and James Madison in *The Federalist* were a
decisive factor in winning acceptance for the
Constitution in the face of that bitterness.   But
for those articles the Union might never have
been achieved; a weight, therefore, seldom accorded to the opinions of statesmen attaches to
those to which expression was given in the
pages of Hamilton's famous periodical.   For of
Hamilton and Madison it may be said that as
their courage was justified by the accomplish-

ment of their immediate purpose in their life-
time, so their political insight was vindicated
by the permanency of that which they had built.

Advocates and opponents of the League of
Nations may alike quarry profitably for
weapons for their armoury in *The Federalist*
(especially in Nos. 9, 15-22 and 41-45).

For those who dislike the idea of a League
of Nations it is indeed a happy hunting-ground.
For it was Hamilton's purpose to persuade the
Thirteen States to abandon in favour of a Federal Union the loose Confederation completed
in 1781. It is not surprising, therefore, to find
that he has many hard things to say of Confederations, and indeed numbers 17 to 20 are devoted to a destructive examination of historical
examples. Amongst other defects in the form
of political organization he instances the following. The commands of the Confederacy, even
when in theory binding on the separate States,
are apt in practice to be mere recommendations
which the States observe or disregard at their
option. Owing to the nature of sovereign power,
there is an eccentric tendency amongst the
lesser sovereignties to fly off from the common

centre. The Union which is intended to preserve peace is in fact the cause or the occasion of constant bickerings, quarrels, and even war. Again the demand for unanimity amongst a number of different wills prevents prompt or effective action, and subjects the essential interests of the whole to the caprice or corruption of a single member. In fine, "the great and radical vice" in the construction of a Confederation is that it creates "the political monster of an *imperium in imperio*" (No. 15). "The important truth," he says elsewhere (No. 20), "is that a sovereignty over sovereigns, a government over governments, a legislation for communities, as contradistinguished from individuals, as it is a solecism in theory, so in practice it is subversive of the order and ends of civil polity, by substituting *violence* in place of *law*, or the destructive *coercion* of the *sword* in place of the mild and salutory *coercion* of the *magistracy*." And Madison (No. 42) speaks of the endeavour "to accomplish impossibilities; to reconcile a partial sovereignty in the Union with complete sovereignty in the States; to subvert a mathematical axiom by taking away a part and letting the whole remain.''

These arguments presented with eloquence and knowledge may at first fill with despair those who see in a League of Nations the only hope for the future of civilization. Yet they will also find in *The Federalist* valuable support and grounds for encouragement. In the first place it is clear that neither Hamilton nor Madison believed in the time-honoured doctrine of the indivisibility of sovereignty. Still more will these ''visionaries'' take courage from the victory and the beneficent results of the victory won by the Federalists over ''the inordinate pride of State importance.'' The American Constitution is the living memorial of the victory won by the fresh and invigorating ideas of young men over the interested, short-sighted and narrow-minded opposition of pedantic older men.

There is another important consideration. When we weigh the views of Hamilton and Madison, we must not lose sight of the difference between their object and ours or between the circumstances in which they were working and those in which we find ourselves. Their object was to create a nation; the object of a League of Nations is, not to create a nation but to create a League between independent nations for certain defined purposes. It is doubtful whether Hamilton would have considered this either absurd or impracticable (*cf.* No. 89). The Federalists were concerned to draw tighter the bonds of union which had already been tied, and to strengthen a co-operation already begun. The European States have not yet reached the "jumping-off point" of the framers of the American Constitution.

Further, since Hamilton's days history shows us modern instances, and of these the greatest is the British Empire. Mr. Hughes, the Prime Minister of Australia, has spoken, not once but many times, of Australia as an independent State; counsel for the Canadian Government has opposed an application before the International Joint Waterways Commission on the ground that the application involved an invasion of *its* treaty-rights,[1] and the War Cabi-

---

[1] *Law Times,* vol. 145, p. 404.

net has recently decided that henceforth communications between the Government of Canada and Great Britain shall go direct instead of through the Colonial Office and the Governor. Metternich said that no sovereign could afford to give away a particle of his sovereignty. Professor Pollard neatly comments :[2] "We may not give it away, but we lease it to the Dominions and get a handsome return." We are, General Smuts has said, "not a State but a community of States and nations . . . a whole world by ourselves consisting of many nations, of many States and all sorts of communities under one flag." Many of the criticisms which Hamilton levelled against Confederacies might be levelled against the fabric of the British "Empire"—a Commonwealth which has proved itself alike in war and peace.

Finally, it is possible that had there been no Confederation in 1781 there would have been no Federal State in 1789. It is no less possible that the League of Nations may prove a stepping-stone, necessary in its day, to some closer

[2] *The Commonwealth at War*, ch. 16, p. 226.

union of the civilized States of the world. For at the moment, as Mr. Lowes Dickinson has said, "the problem is to find the greatest measure of organization which the state of feeling and intelligence after the war will tolerate."[1] Few would suggest that the League of Nations in its present form is the final solution: we most of us believe that it is the right step to take next.

APPENDIX II

SCHEMES FOR A LEAGUE OF NATIONS[1]

(1)

THE PLATFORM OF THE LEAGUE OF NATIONS SOCIETY

(1, Central Buildings, Westminster, S.W. 1)

The objects of the Society shall be to advocate :—

1. That a Treaty shall be made as soon as possible whereby as many States as are willing shall form a League binding themselves to use

---

[1] Full particulars of five other schemes will be found in L. S. Woolf's *The Framework of a Lasting Peace.* The late Lord Parker of Waddington propounded a working scheme in his speech in the House of Lords on March 19th, 1918. It was not fully reported in the Press and must be read in the official Parliamentary Debates. There is an admirable account of earlier plans with the same object, such as the " Grand Design " in Lorimer's *Institutes of the Law of Nations,* Bk. v., ch. 7, and Professor Pollard published during the summer a brightly-written pamphlet —*The League of Nations in History*—on the same subject. An English translation of Rousseau's *Extrait du Projet de Paix perpetuelle de M. L'Abbé de St. Pierre* was issued by Messrs. Constable in 1917 under the title, *A Lasting Peace and the State of War.*

peaceful methods for dealing with all disputes arising among them.

2. That such methods shall be as follows :—

(*a*) All disputes arising out of questions of international law or the interpretation of Treaties shall be referred to the Hague Court of Arbitration, or some other Judicial Tribunal, whose decisions shall be final, and shall be carried into effect by the parties concerned.

(*b*) All other disputes shall be referred to and investigated and reported upon by a Council of Inquiry and Conciliation, the Council to be representative of the States which form the League.

3. That the States which are members of the League shall unite in any action necessary for ensuring that every member shall abide by the terms of the Treaty; and in particular shall jointly use forthwith both their economic and military forces against any one of their number that goes to war, or commits acts of hostility against another, before any question arising shall be submitted as provided in the foregoing Articles.

4. That the States which are members of the League shall make provision for mutual defence, diplomatic, economic and military, in the event of any of them being attacked by a State, not a member of the League, which refuses to submit the case to an appropriate Tribunal or Council.

5. That conferences between the members of the League shall be held from time to time to consider international matters of a general character, and to formulate and codify rules of international law, which, unless some member shall signify its dissent within a stated period, shall hereafter govern in the decisions of the Judicial Tribunal mentioned in Article 2 (*a*).

6. That any civilized State desiring to join the League shall be admitted to membership.

(2)

THE PLATFORM OF THE LEAGUE TO ENFORCE PEACE

(507, 5th Avenue, New York City, U.S.A.)

We believe it to be desirable for the United States to join a League of Nations binding the signatories to the following :—

First: All justiciable questions arising between the signatory Powers, not settled by negotiation, shall, subject to the limitations of treaties, be submitted to a judicial tribunal for hearing and judgment, both upon the merits and upon any issue as to its jurisdiction of the question.

Second: All other questions arising between the signatories and not settled by negotiation, shall be submitted to a Council of Conciliation for hearing, consideration and recommendation.

Third: The signatory Powers shall jointly use forthwith both their economic and military forces against any one of their number that goes to war, or commits acts of hostility, against another of the signatories before any question arising shall be submitted as provided in the foregoing.

Fourth: Conferences between the signatory Powers shall be held from time to time to formulate and codify rules of international law, which, unless some signatory shall signify its dissent within a stated period, shall thereafter govern in the decisions of the Judicial Tribunal mentioned in Article One.

APPENDIX III.

PRESIDENT WILSON'S PROGRAMME[1]

28th May, 1916 : Washington

ONLY when the great nations of the world have reached some sort of agreement as to what they hold to be fundamental for their common interest, and as to some feasible method of acting in concert when any nation or group of nations seeks to disturb those fundamental things, can we feel that civilization is, at last, in a way of justifying its existence and claiming to be finally established.

It is clear that nations must in the future be governed by the same high code of honour that we demand of individuals.

[1] This collection of extracts from President Wilson's speeches and notes is limited to the more important pronouncements bearing immediately upon the topic of this book. It does not profess to illustrate the whole of the President's Peace Terms or of his programme for the future.

Repeated utterances of the leading statesmen of most of the great nations now engaged in war have made it plain that their thought has come to this—that the principle of public right must henceforth take precedence over the individual interests of particular nations, and that the nations of the world must in some way band themselves together to see that that right prevails as against any sort of selfish aggression; that henceforth alliance must not be set up against alliance, understanding against understanding, but that there must be a common agreement for a common object, and that at the heart of that common object must lie the inviolable rights of peoples and of mankind.

In the dealings of nations with one another arbitrary force must be rejected, and we must move forward to the thought of the modern world, the thought of which peace is the very atmosphere.

We believe these fundamental things:

First, that every people has a right to choose the sovereignty under which they shall live.

Second, that the small States of the world have a right to enjoy the same respect for their sovereignty and for their territorial integrity that great and powerful nations expect and insist upon.

And third, that the world has a right to be free from every disturbance of its peace that has its origin in aggression and disregard of the rights of peoples and nations.

So sincerely do we believe in these things that I am sure that I speak the mind and wish of the people of America when I say that the United States is willing to become a partner in any feasible association of nations formed in order to realize these objects and make them secure against violation.

There is nothing that the United States wants for itself that any other nation has. We are willing, on the contrary, to limit ourselves along with them to a prescribed course of duty and respect for the rights of others, which will check any selfish passion of our own as it will check any aggressive impulse of theirs.

If it should ever be our privilege to suggest or initiate a movement for peace among the nations now at war, I am sure that the people of the United States would wish their Government to move along the line of a universal association of the nations to maintain the inviolate security of the highway of the seas for the common and unhindered use of all the nations of the world, and to prevent any war begun either contrary to treaty covenants or without warning, and full submission of the causes to the opinion of the world—a virtual guarantee of territorial integrity and political independence.

I feel that the world is even now upon the eve of a great consummation, when some common force will be brought into existence which shall safeguard right as the first and most fundamental interest of all peoples and all governments, when coercion shall be summoned not to the service of political ambition or selfish hostility, but to the service of a common order, a common justice, and a common peace.

God grant that the dawn of that day of frank dealing and of settled peace, concord, and cooperation may be near at hand!

2nd September, 1916

No nation can any longer remain neutral as against any wilful disturbance of the peace of the world. The effects of war can no longer be confined to the areas of battle. No nation stands wholly apart in interest when the life and interest of all nations are thrown into confusion and peril. If hopeful and generous intercourse is to be renewed, if the healing and helpful arts of life are indeed to be revived when peace comes again, a new atmosphere of justice and friendship must be generated by means the world has never tried before. The nations of the world must unite in joint guarantees that, whatever is done to disturb the whole world's life, must first be tested in the court of the whole world's opinion before it is attempted to secure this end.

5th October, 1916

We want all the world to know that Americans are ready in years to come to lend our force without stint to the preservation of peace in the interests of mankind. The world is no longer divided into little circles of interest. The world no longer consists of neighbourhoods. The whole is linked together in a common life and interest such as humanity never saw before, and the starting of wars can never again be a private and individual matter for nations.[2]

22nd January, 1917 : Washington

In every discussion of the peace that must end this war it is taken for granted that peace must be followed by definite concert of the Powers which will make it virtually impossible that any such catastrophe should ever overwhelm us again. Every lover of mankind, every sane and thoughtful man, must take that for granted. . . .

It will be absolutely necessary that a force be created as a guarantor of the permanency of the settlement so much greater[3] than the force of any nation now engaged or any alliance hitherto formed or projected, that no nation, no probable combination of nations, could face or withstand it. If the peace presently to be made is to endure, it must be a peace made secure by the organized major force of mankind. . . .

---

[2] *Quære :* Does President Wilson desire to make acceptance of the decisions of the League on non-justiciable questions enforceable by the power of the League?

[3] *Quære :* Absolutely or relatively? In view of President Wilson's statements on disarmament presumably the latter.

The equality of nations upon which peace must be founded, if it is to last, must be an equality of rights; the guarantees exchanged must neither recognize nor imply a difference between big nations and small; between those that are powerful and those that are weak. Right must be based upon the common strength, not upon the individual strength, of the nations upon whose concert peace will depend.

Equality of territory or of resources there, of course, cannot be; nor any other sort of equality not gained in the ordinary peaceful and legitimate development of the peoples themselves. But no one asks or expects more than an equality of rights. Mankind is looking now for freedom of life, not for equipoises of power.

And there is a deeper thing involved than even equality of right among organized nations.

No peace can last, or ought to last, which does not recognize and accept the principle that Governments derive all their just powers from the consent of the governed, and that no right anywhere exists to hand peoples about from potentate to potentate as if they were property. . . .

So far as practicable, moreover, every great people now struggling towards a full development of its resources and of its powers should be assured a direct outlet to the great highways of the sea.

Where this cannot be done by the cession of territory, it no doubt can be done by the neutralization of direct rights of way under the general guarantee which will assure the peace itself. With a right comity of arrangement no nation need be shut away from free access to the open paths of the world's commerce.

And the paths of the sea must alike in law and in fact be free. The freedom of the seas is the *sine qua non* of peace, equality, and cooperation.

No doubt a somewhat radical reconsideration of many of the rules of international practice hitherto thought to be established may be necessary in order to make the seas indeed free and common in practically all circumstances for the use of mankind; but the motive for such changes is convincing and compelling. There can be no trust or intimacy between the peoples of the world without them. The free, constant, unthreatened intercourse of nations is an essential part of the process of peace and of development. It need not be difficult either to define or to secure the freedom of the seas if the Governments of the world sincerely desire to come to an agreement concerning it.

It is a problem closely connected with the limitation of naval armaments and the co-operation of the navies of the world in keeping the seas at once free and safe, and the question of limiting naval armaments opens the wider and perhaps more difficult question of the limitation of armies and of all programmes of military preparation. Difficult and delicate as these questions are, they must be faced with the utmost candour and decided in a spirit of real accommodation, if peace is to come with healing in its wings, and come to stay. Peace cannot be had without concession and sacrifice.

There can be no sense of safety and equality among the nations if great and preponderating armaments are henceforth to continue here and there to be built up and maintained. The statesmen of the world must plan for peace, and nations must adjust and accommodate their policy to it, as they have planned for war and made ready for pitiless contest and rivalry.

The question of armaments whether on land or sea is the most immediately and intensely practical question connected with the future fortunes of nations and of mankind.

5th March, 1917 : *Washington*

These, therefore, are the things we shall stand for, whether in war or peace—that all nations are equally interested in the peace of the world and in the political stability of free peoples, and are equally responsible for their maintenance, that the essential principle of peace is the actual equality of nations in all matters of right or privilege, that peace cannot securely or justly rest upon an armed balance of power, that Governments derive all their just powers from the consent of the governed, and that no other Powers should be supported by the common thought, purpose, or powers of the family of nations, that the seas should be equally free and safe for the use of all peoples under rules set up by common agreement and consent, and that so far as is practicable they should be accessible to all upon equal terms; that national armaments should be limited to the necessities of national order and domestic safety; that the community of interest and power upon which peace will henceforth depend imposes upon each nation the duty of seeing to it that all influences proceeding from its own citizens meant to encourage or assist revolution in other States should be sternly and effectually suppressed and prevented.

I need not argue these principles to you, my fellow-countrymen. They are your own—part and parcel of your own thinking, of your own motive in affairs. They spring up native amongst us. Upon this, as upon a platform of purpose and action, we can stand together, and it is imperative that we should stand together.

3rd April, 1917 : *Washington*

Our object . . . is to vindicate the principles of peace and justice in the life of the world as against selfish autocratic power, and to set up amongst really free and self-governed peoples of the world such a concert of purpose and action as will henceforth ensure the observance of these principles.

Neutrality is no longer feasible or desirable where the peace of the world is involved and the freedom of its peoples, and the menace to that peace and freedom lies in the existence of autocratic Governments backed by organized force which is controlled wholly by their will and not by the will of their people.

We have seen the last of neutrality in such circumstances. We are at the beginning of an age in which it will be insisted that the same standards of conduct and responsibility for wrong done shall be observed among nations and their Governments that are observed among individual citizens of civilized States. . . .

A stedfast concert for peace can never be maintained except by the partnership of democratic nations. No autocratic Government could be trusted to keep faith within it or observe its covenants. There must be a league of honour and partnership of opinion. Intrigue would eat its vitals away. Plottings by inner circles, who would plan what they would and render an account to no one, would be corruption seated at its very heart. Only free peoples can hold their purpose and their honour steady to the common end and prefer the interests of mankind to any narrow interest of their own. . . .

We are now about to accept the gage of battle with this natural foe to liberty, and shall, if necessary, spend the whole force of the nation to check and nullify its pretensions and its power. We are glad, now that we see facts with no veil of false pretence about them, to fight thus for the ultimate peace of the world, for the liberation of its peoples—the German peoples included—the rights of nations great and small, and the privilege of men everywhere to choose their way of life and obedience. The world must be safe for democracy. Its peace must be planted upon trusted foundations of political liberty. . . .

Civilization itself seems to be in the balance; but right is more precious than peace, and we shall fight for the things which we have always carried nearest our hearts—for democracy, for the right of those who submit to authority to

have a voice in their own government, for the
rights and liberties of small nations, for the
universal dominion of right by such a concert
of free peoples as will bring peace and safety
to all nations and make the world itself at last
free.

To such a task we can dedicate our lives,
our fortunes, everything we are, everything we
have, with the pride of those who know the day
has come when America is privileged to spend
her blood and might for the principles that
gave her birth, and the happiness and peace
which she has treasured. God helping her,
she can do no other.

30th August, 1917 : *Reply to the Pope's Note*

Responsible statesmen must now everywhere
see, if they never saw before, that no peace can
rest securely upon political restrictions meant
to benefit some nations and cripple or embar-
rass others, upon vindictive action of any sort,
or any kind of revenge or deliberate injury.
The American people have suffered intolerable
wrongs at the hands of the Imperial German
Government, but they desire no reprisal upon

the German people, who have themselves suffered all things in this war which they did not
choose.   They believe that peace should rest
upon the rights of peoples, not the rights of
Governments, the rights of peoples great or
small, weak or powerful, their equal right to
freedom and security and self-government, and
to a participation upon fair terms in the economic opportunities of the world, the German
peoples, of course, included, if they will accept
equality and not seek domination. . . .

The purposes of the United States in this war
are known to the whole world—to every people
to whom the truth has been permitted to come.
They do not need to be stated again.   We seek
no material advantages of any kind.   We believe that the intolerable wrongs done in this
war by the furious and brutal power of the Imperial German Government, ought to be re-
paired, but not at the expense of the sovereignty
of any people—rather in vindication of the sovereignty both of those that are weak and of those
that are strong.   Punitive damages, the dis-
memberment of empires, the establishment of
selfish and exclusive economic leagues, we

deem inexpedient and in the end worse than futile, no proper basis for a peace of any kind, least of all for an enduring peace. That must be based upon justice and fairness and the common rights of mankind.

4th December, 1917.

We do not wish in any way to impair or to re-arrange the Austro-Hungarian Empire. It is no affair of ours what they do with their own life, either industrially or politically. We do not purpose or desire to dictate to them in any way. We only desire to see that their affairs are left in their own hands in all matters, great or small. . . . And our attitude and purpose with regard to Germany herself are of a like kind. We intend no wrong against the German Empire, no interference with her internal affairs. We should deem either the one or the other absolutely unjustifiable, absolutely contrary to the principles we have professed to live by and to hold most sacred throughout our life as a nation. . . .

The worst that can happen to the detriment of the German people is this—that if they should still after the war is over continue to be obliged to live under ambitious and intriguing masters interested to disturb the peace of the world, or classes of men whom the other peoples of the world could not trust, it might be impossible to admit them to the partnership of nations which must henceforth guarantee the world's peace.   That partnership must be a partnership of peoples, not a mere partnership of Governments. It might be impossible also in such untoward circumstances to admit Germany to the free economic intercourse which must inevitably spring out of the other partnership of a real peace.   But there would be no aggression in that, and such a situation, inevitable because of distrust, would in the very nature of things sooner or later cure itself by processes which would assuredly set in.

8th January, 1918 : *Washington*
(The Fourteen Points)

What we demand in this war, therefore, is nothing peculiar to ourselves.   It is that the world be made fit and safe to live in, and particularly that it be made safe for every peace-loving nation which, like our own, wishes to live its own free life, determine its own institutions, be assured of justice and fair dealing by the other peoples of the world, as against force and selfish aggression. All the peoples of the world are in effect partners in this interest, and for our own part we see very clearly that unless justice be done to others it will not be done to us.

The programme of the world's peace, therefore, is our programme, and that programme, the only possible one as we see it, is this:—

I.—Open covenants of peace openly arrived at, after which there shall be no private international understandings of any kind, but diplomacy shall proceed always frankly and in the public view.

II.—Absolute freedom of navigation upon the seas outside territorial waters alike in peace and in war except as the seas may be closed in whole or in part by international action for the enforcement of international covenants.

III.—The removal, so far as possible, of all economic barriers and the establishment of an equality of trade conditions among all the nations consenting to the peace and associating themselves for its maintenance.

IV.—Adequate guarantees given and taken that national armaments will be reduced to the lowest point consistent with domestic safety.

V.—A free, open-minded and absolutely impartial adjustment of all colonial claims based upon a strict observance of the principle that in determining all such questions of sovereignty the interests of the populations concerned must have equal weight with the equitable claims of the Government whose title is to be determined. . . .

XIV.—A general association of nations must be formed under specific covenants for the purpose of affording mutual guarantees of political and territorial independence for great and small States alike.

11th February, 1918 : *Washington*

Whatever affects the peace affects mankind, and nothing settled by military force, if settled wrong, is settled at all.   It will presently have to be re-opened. . . .

The principles to be applied are these:—

. . . Second, that peoples and provinces are not to be bartered about from sovereignty to sovereignty as if they were mere chattels and pawns in a game, even the great game now for ever discredited of the balance of power; but that

Third, every territorial settlement involved in this war must be made in the interest and for the benefit of the populations concerned, and not as a part of any mere adjustment or compromise of claims amongst rival States.

4th July, 1918

The past and the present are in deadly grapple, and the peoples of the world are being done to death between them. . . .

These are the ends for which the associated peoples of the world are fighting, and which must be conceded them before there can be peace. . . .

Third, the consent of all nations to be governed in their conduct towards each other by the same principles of honour and of respect for the common law of civilized society that govern the individual citizens of all modern States in their relations with one another, to the end that all promises and covenants may be sacredly observed, no private plots or conspiracies hatched, no selfish injuries wrought with impunity, and a mutual trust established upon the handsome foundation of a mutual respect for right.

Fourth, the establishment of an organization of peace which shall make it certain that the combined power of free nations will check every invasion of right and serve to make peace and justice the more secure by affording a definite tribunal of opinion to which all must submit, and by which every international readjustment that cannot be amically agreed upon by the peoples directly concerned shall be sanctioned.

These great objects can be put into a single sentence. What we seek is the reign of law based upon the consent of the governed and sustained by the organized opinion of mankind.

27th September, 1918: New York

We accepted the issues of the war as facts, not as any group of men either here or elsewhere had defined them, and we can accept no outcome which does not squarely meet and settle them.

The issues are these :—

Shall the military power of any nation, or group of nations, be suffered to determine the fortunes of peoples over whom they have no right to rule except the right of force?

Shall strong nations be free to wrong weak nations and make them subject to their purposes and interest?

Shall peoples be ruled and dominated, even in their own internal affairs, by arbitrary and irresponsible force, or by their own will and choice?

Shall there be a common standard of right and privilege for all peoples and nations, or shall the strong do as they will, and the weak suffer without redress?

Shall the assertion of right be haphazard and by casual alliance, or shall there be a common concert to oblige the observance of common rights?

No man, no group of men, chose these to be the issues of the struggle. They are the issues of it.

If it be, in deed and in truth, the common object of the Governments associated against Germany and of the nations whom they govern, as I believe it to be, to achieve by the coming settlements a secure and lasting peace, it will be necessary that all who sit down at the peace table shall come ready and willing to pay the price, the only price, that will procure it; and ready and willing also to create in some virile fashion the only instrumentality by which it can be made certain that the agreements of the peace will be honoured and fulfilled. That price is impartial justice in every item of the settlement, no matter whose interest is crossed; and not only impartial justice, but also the satisfaction of the several peoples whose fortunes are dealt with. That indispensable instrumentality is a League of Nations formed under covenants that will be inefficacious without such an instrumentality by which the peace of the world can be guaranteed. Peace will rest in part upon the word of outlaws, and only upon that word. For Germany will have to redeem her character, not by what happens at the peace table but by what follows.

And as I see it, the constitution of that League of Nations and the clear definition of its objects must be a part, in a sense the most essential part, of the peace settlement itself. It cannot be formed now. If formed now it would be merely a new alliance confined to the nations associated against a common enemy. . . .

But these general terms do not disclose the whole matter. Some details are needed to make them sound less like a thesis and more like a practical programme. These, then, are some of the particulars, and I state them with the greater confidence because I can state them authoritatively as representing this Government's interpretation of its own duty with regard to peace :—

First, the impartial justice meted out must involve no discrimination between those to whom we wish to be just and those to whom we do not wish to be just. It must be a justice that has no favourites and knows no standards but the equal rights of the several peoples concerned.

Second, no special or separate interest of any single nation or any group of nations can be made the basis of any part of the settlement which is not consistent with the common interest of all.

Third, there can be no leagues or alliances or special covenants and understandings within the general and common family of the League of Nations.

Fourth, and more specifically, there can be no special, selfish economic combinations within the League, and no employment of any form of economic boycott or exclusion, except as the power of economic penalty, by exclusion from the markets of the world, may be vested in the League of Nations itself as a means of discipline and control.

Fifth, all international agreements and treaties of every kind must be made known in their entirety to the rest of the world. . . .

In the same sentence in which I say that the United States will enter into no special arrangements or understandings with particular nations let me say also that the United States is prepared to assume its full share of responsibility for the maintenance of the common covenants and understandings upon which peace must henceforth rest.

We still read Washington's immortal warning against " entangling alliances " with full comprehension and an answering purpose. But only special and limited alliances entangle; and we recognize and accept the duty of a new day in which we are permitted to hope for a general alliance, which will avoid entanglements and clear the air of the world for common understandings and the maintenance of common rights.

APPENDIX IV

VISCOUNT GREY'S PROPOSALS
(From his speech at Westminster, 10th October, 1918)

LET me take one or two points which we ought to have definitely settled in our minds in regard to the working of the League of Nations. How is it going to affect the fiscal question, for in stance? There, again, I take what I understand to be President Wilson's attitude the other day. He says, "No economic boycott within the League of Nations," but he leaves, or I understand he contemplates leaving, each individual member of the League of Nations—each Empire, each State, each Republic, whatever it may be—free within the League to settle its own fiscal question for itself. We may have our own, and we probably shall have our own, fights here on the fiscal question. It will be very surprising if there is not some discussion and some controversy, but with regard to the League of Nations you may keep that outside the question of the League, and settle it for yourselves in your own way; but having settled your fiscal system, you must recognize that in a League of Nations you will be bound to apply that fiscal system, whatever it may be, equally to all the other members of the League. You won't be able to differentiate amongst them. That I understand to be the principle laid down by President Wilson, and that is the principle which certainly commends itself to me. That, I think, is a principle which must be accepted if the League of Nations is to be a League that will guarantee the peace of the world.

There is another important point in connexion with the fiscal side of the League of Nations. During this war there has been brought into existence an economic boycott of the enemy countries. I am told it has been very effective. The machinery for it is in existence. In my opinion the Allies who have brought that machinery into existence should keep that machinery ready as part of the League of Nations, and if in future years an individual member of the League of Nations breaks the covenant of that League, that economic weapon is going to be a most powerful weapon in the hands of the League as a whole.   I think that economic weapon is most valuable as a future influence in keeping the peace and in deterring nations who have come into the League of Nations from breaking any covenant in the League.   It will be a most valuable influence for that purpose, but then if it is to be a valuable influence for that purpose you must not bring it into existence before the purpose has arisen, or before there has been some breach of the covenant.

Well, now I come to another thorny and difficult subject connected with the League of Nations, the question of what is called disarmament.   I have tried as far as I can to get the fiscal difficulties put as clearly as possible so that they will not stand in the way of a League of Nations.   You have got to handle also this question of disarmament very carefully.   You will have many apprehensions in this country that somehow or other a League of Nations is going to put us in a disadvantageous position, where we may be, by bad faith or otherwise, put in a position in which we are not sufficiently capable of defending ourselves. I think you have got to go very carefully in your League of Nations with regard to definite proposals that may be suggested or adopted with regard to what is called disarmament. One thing I do not mind saying. Before this war the expenditure on armaments, naval and military, had been going up by leaps and bounds. Germany had been forcing the pace in both. She has led the way up the hill in increasing expenditure on armaments. She must lead the way down the hill. That that is a first condition from our point of view goes without saying—there can be no talk of disarmament until Germany, the great armer, has disarmed.

But then I think we must go further than that. I think the League of Nations might insist upon each Government which is a member of the League of Nations becoming itself responsible for the amount of armaments made in its own country. Your difficulty now is that in a given country there may be a vast number of ships of war, guns, and munitions of war being made, and the Government may say, ''Oh, these are being made by private firms for other countries, and we have nothing to do with them.'' I do not see why it should be impossible for Governments to agree that they will keep that matter in their own hands, that they will give the fullest public information and the fullest opportunities for acquiring information as to the actual amount of what are called armaments being constructed, or available in each country at any given time. I do not see why that should not be done in the future. And if that were done, and you found some Governments beginning to force the pace in armaments, I rather think that you would find the matter being brought before the League of Nations, and a discussion would arise as to whether it was time to bring the economic weapon into use before things went further. The League of Nations may have considerable power, provided the Governments admit responsibility with regard to the amount of armaments being constructed.

But remember, even so, that you will never, by any regulations you may make about armaments, dispose completely of the question. Supposing to-morrow, or after the war is over, the financial pressure were so great, and the feeling that another war was remote was so strong, that ships of war, munitions of war, ceased to be constructed in the world at large, and those now in existence were allowed to lapse or become obsolete until armaments had disappeared in the form in which we know them. Supposing all that happened, you would not have settled the question, because then the potential weapons of war would be your merchant ships and commercial aeroplanes. All those things will be developed after the war, and in the construction of those things you can have no limitation—they must go on being built by private firms. You cannot limit the merchant ships or the amount of commercial aeroplanes to be built, and the fewer the armaments, fighting aeroplanes, and ships of war in the ordinarily accepted sense, the more important potentially as weapons of war become the things you use in commerce, your ships, aeroplanes, and chemicals of all kinds. Well, then, is not the moral of it all this, that the one thing which is going to produce disarmament in the world is a sense of security?   And it is because I believe that a League of Nations may produce, and will produce, that sense of security in the world at large which will make disarmament— disarmament in the sense of the reduction of armaments—a reality and not a sham, that is one reason for advocating a League of Nations in order that we may have that sense of security.

Now I come to one other point.   We must with a League of Nations be sure that in all these ideals which have been put forward—that in putting forward these ideals we have been saying what we mean and meaning what we said.   When the time comes, and the war has been brought to a successful conclusion, we must make it clear that the object of the League of Nations movement has been to get a League of Nations formed—and that is clear in every speech President Wilson has made about it— into which you can get Germany, and not formed in order that you may find a pretext for keeping Germany out.   On the other hand, your League of Nations must not be a sham, and you must have no nation in it which is not sincere. That means that you must have every Government in the League of Nations representing a free people, a free people which is as thoroughly convinced as are the countries who now desire the League of Nations, of the objects of the League, and are thoroughly determined to carry out those objects in all sincerity. That you must do. When you come to define democracy—real democracy, and not sham democracy —I would call to mind that it is not a question of defining special conditions. We here, under the form of constitutional monarchy, are as democratic as any republic in the world; and I trust the people of this country to do what Mr. John Morley, as he then was, once said with regard to a Jingo. He said, "I cannot define a Jingo, but I know one when I see him." I believe the people of this country are perfectly capable, though they may not wish to define what constitutes a democracy, of knowing a democracy when they see it. As President Wilson has repeatedly said, you can trust no Government which does not come to you with the credentials that it exists with the confidence of the people behind it, and is responsible to that people, and to no one else.

But there are one or two things more which I think may be done by a League of Nations, and which are very important. Supposing the League once formed, the treaty signed, the treaty binding the nations composing the League to settle any disputes that may arise between them by some method other than that of war, and each of them undertaking an obligation that, if any nation does break that covenant, they will use all the forces at their disposal against that nation which has so broken it. Supposing that done, I think more use can be made of the League of Nations than that. There is work for it to do from day to day which may be very valuable. I do not see why the League of Nations, once formed, should necessarily be idle. I do not see why it should not arrange for an authority and an international force at its disposal which should act as police act in individual countries. It sometimes happens, for instance, when a wrong is done for which some backward country, very often a small backward country, will not give redress.

Its Government perhaps lacks authority, and you have seen from time to time that in such circumstances a stronger nation has resorted to force and seized a port or brought some other pressure of that kind to bear. And then you had the jealousy of other nations existing, thinking that the stronger nation, in seeking redress, is in some way pursuing its own interests. I think these cases might be settled, if force be necessary, by a League of Nations if it had an international force at its disposal, without giving rise to the suspicions and jealousies of certain political aims being pursued.

Another thing it may do. It may possibly do a great deal with regard to Labour. Mr. Barnes said that his presence in the War Cabinet was temporary, I think he said accidental and embarrassing. Well, public positions are generally embarrassing, but I doubt Mr. Barnes' position being either temporary or accidental. I think Labour is undoubtedly going to take a larger and more prominent share in the Governments than it has done before. It may be that here, as elsewhere, we shall have Labour Governments. Well, now, I put this forward only tentatively. Labour now has its international conferences, but they are unofficial. Is it not possible that as Labour takes a larger and more prominent share in government it may find a League of Nations useful as a means of giving a more official character to these international consultations in the interest of Labour which independent Labour has already encouraged and taken so much part in?

Then I would give you another suggestion, and it is the last on this point. There are countries of the world, independent nations, but more loosely organized, or for one reason or another incapable through their Governments of managing their own affairs effectively from the point of view of those other more highly organized countries who wish to trade with them, and they want assistance in the shape of officials from the more highly organized countries. A great example of that is the Maritime Customs Service in China, formed by the Chinese Government under Sir Robert Hart, and working as an international force, I believe, with the approval of the whole world in the interests of China and of the world generally. Well, that was done—I give it as an illustration—for the Chinese Government, but there are other countries in the world where that sort of thing is even more needed, and it is very seldom done because the weaker country which needs it is afraid of admitting foreign officials, for fear they may have some political design and interest. It is discouraged because individual countries are each jealous of one another getting a footing in some of these more backward countries, through officials. But, if you had your League of Nations, what was done for China in the form of an International Customs Service, to the benefit of China and the whole world, might be done in other countries which need that sort of assistance. What has prevented it being done is the jealousy the stronger States have of one another and the fear of the weaker nation that it is going to admit political influence and sacrifice independence. But if this were done on the authority of a League of Nations there would be much less chance of these jealousies, and much less chance of weaker nations being afraid of ulterior designs, and the trade of the world and that of individual States might benefit enormously by the confidence with which that assistance could be given if given under a League of Nations and not by one individual country or group of countries.

For Product Safety Concerns and Information please contact our EU
representative GPSR@taylorandfrancis.com
Taylor & Francis Verlag GmbH, Kaufingerstraße 24, 80331 München, Germany